Ant Farms
The Ultimate Formicarium
Handbook

Detailed Step-by-Step Guide to Setting Up a Thriving Ant Colony

By Angela Hayes

Foreword

Keeping ants is a mesmerizing experience. Although not obvious as a choice of pet, they are truly spectacular. An formicarium / ant farm allows you to observe these incredibly industrious creatures up close.

This book will enable you to understand the ant's unique and fascinating behavior and appreciate their complex social organization. You will learn how to set up an ant colony enclosure (known as a formicarium) and how to ensure that your ants thrive.

Foreword

Raising ants is far from owning a regular pet. Having your own formicarium / ant farm provides you with an intriguing glimpse into the wonderful civilization of ants.

Just like humans, ants build structures, search for food, defend their societies and manage waste. To achieve this way of life, like us, they must be extremely well organized. And yet, unlike the human world, there is no centralized control. Surely, we can learn from these hardworking and ordered creatures

Additionally, these captivating insects are comparatively low maintenance.

Unsurprisingly, ant farms are becoming increasingly popular with both adults and children. This handbook has been designed to help you become the best ant keeper that you can be.

Equally importantly, by providing you with a background on ants and their behavior, you will understand so much more about what is happening in your ant farm – and you will appreciate them even more because of it!

Guaranteed that after reading this book and setting up your own ant farm, you will no longer be able walk past an ant without noticing. You will be wondering about the colony it has come from and what role this ant plays. The more you know about ants, the more captivating and intriguing they are.

Foreword

Table of Contents

Foreword 2

Table of Contents 5

Chapter One - Introduction to Ant Farms 11

    Meet the Ants.. 11

    So Many Ants! 12

    Why Keep Ants?.. 13

    Understanding the Ant Colony.................... 15

    The Queen Ant 15

    Nanitics... 17

    Worker Ants.. 17

    Soldier Ants.. 18

    Winged Princess 19

    Winged Drone 20

Chapter Two – Ants Under the Microscope 22

    External Ant Anatomy 22

    Outside the Head 23

    Exterior of the Thorax.................................. 27

    External of the Abdomen 28

    Internal Ant Anatomy 28

Chapter Three – Exploring Ant Behavior 31

Table of Contents

The Nuptial Flight 31

Life Cycle of the Ant 32

How Ants Communicate 35

Defense Systems 37

Protecting against Pathogens 38

Foraging for Food 39

Joining Forces 40

Sharing Food with the Colony 42

How Ants Learn 42

Monomorphic and Polymorphic Ant Colonies 44

Chapter Four – Getting Ready for your Ant Farm 46

Starting Out 46

Basic Ant Necessities 47

The Formicarium 48

Beginning with a Test Tube 49

Test Tube Nest Set-Up 51

Chapter Five – Sourcing Your Ants 54

Ways to Source Ants 54

Purchasing Ants 56

Collecting Worker Ants 56

Capturing your own Queen Ant 59

Identifying Queen Ants that have Mated 62

Table of Contents

Global Ant Nursery Project 63

Chapter Six – History of Ant Farms and their Rise in
Popularity 64

Charles Janet 64

Frank Eugene Austin 64

Milton Levine 65

Ant Farms Today 66

Sand Based Ant Farms 67

Gel Based Ant Farms 68

Chapter Seven – Introducing the Ants 71

Here Comes the Queen 71

Differences Among Queens 72

Fully-Claustral 73

Semi-Claustral 74

Social Parasites 75

Waiting for Eggs 76

Nanitic Worker Ants 77

Chapter Eight – Caring for an Fledgling Colony 78

Feeding the Workers 78

Sugar Water 79

Honeydew Surrogate 79

Adding a Foraging Area 82

Table of Contents

How Much Food?... 82

A Moldy Test Tube 83

Chapter Nine - Avoid Escaping Ants..................................... 85

Containment 85

Securing the Habitat 86

Talcum Powder 88

Vaseline and Oils.. 89

Fluon 90

Moats... 90

Using a Lid 91

Encourage your Ants to Stay Put................................... 93

Chapter Ten – Managing your Formicarium 94

The Ant Farm... 94

Understanding the Ant Nest 99

Ants Building Nests 100

Controlling the Nest's Environment 101

Moving from the Test Tube to the New Formicarium 102

Building up the Colony 104

Feeding the Colony 104

Chapter Eleven - Humidity and Temperature................... 107

Optimum Humidity.. 107

Table of Contents

Adjusting Humidity Levels 108

How Feeding is Connected to Humidity Levels 110

The Problem with Too Much Humidity 110

The Problem with Too Little Humidity 111

Optimum Temperature 112

Chapter Twelve – Different Ant Species........................... 113

Which Species to Choose 113

Lasius Niger 114

Camponotus.. 118

Tetramorium 123

Myrmica Rubra... 129

Formica fusca 134

Identifying Ants 138

Chapter Thirteen – A Growing Colony 139

Suitable Nest Size 139

Winged Ants 140

Double the Queens? 142

Encouraging the Colony to Expand 142

Heat Pads.. 143

Warm Location 143

Nourishment.. 144

Providing Water 145

Table of Contents

Expected Lifespan 146

Chapter Fourteen – Ants during the Winter 148

Ants that Hibernate.. 148

Allowing your Ants to Hibernate 149

Keeping Ants Cool in the Winter.............................. 149

Chapter Fifteen – Amazing Ant Trivia 151

Chapter Sixteen – Afterword................................... 159

Glossary 161

Index.. 173

Chapter One - Introduction to Ant Farms

Meet the Ants

There are thousands of different ant species – incredibly more than 12,000 all over the world.

Ants existed in the Cretaceous period - about 99 million years ago. This is long before the dinosaurs became extinct at 65 million years.

Around 92 million years ago, seven ants from four different species were encased in amber in what is known today as New Jersey. Dr. David Grimaldi of the American Museum of Natural History found these little fossils in 1998.

These fossils proved very important in our understanding of the evolution of ants. The fossils indicate that ants were well established by this time – to have reached at least four distinct species at that time.

The fossils also show that the ants existed within a social structure at this time. This makes it very likely that ants are the first insects to have complex social structures. They were building their own cities even before the dinosaurs became extinct!

Chapter One - Introduction to Ant Farms

Ants evolved from wasp-like ancestors. The rise of flowering plants enabled the ants to diversify.

So Many Ants!

In our world today, ants are the most populous living creatures.

Despite their tiny size, they have the largest biomass of any other animal. In other words, if all the ants came together and got weighed, they would be heavier than even the combined weight of the entire human population!

Paleontologists believe that there was a remarkable boom in their population sometime around 50 million years ago. There is no explanation for this enormous swell in numbers.

Why Keep Ants?

Ants are remarkably complex creatures who operate within a highly developed social system. The hobby of maintaining ant colonies is increasing in popularity – and it is easy to understand why.

You will be able to watch up close, the way that ant colony functions as a unit. Their industriousness is truly fascinating and will be a constant source of entertainment.

A formicarium or ant farm is a vivarium which is designed principally for the study of ant colonies and how ants behave. Those who study ant behavior are known as myrmecologists. The ant vivarium is an enclosure for keeping and raising ants.

Keeping a formicarium – or ant farm – is a wonderful hobby for ant enthusiasts – whether you are experienced or a real beginner.

Additionally, once your formicarium is operational, it is extremely low maintenance. Perfect for the busy lives we all tend to lead. Ant farms are undoubtedly suitable for both adults and children.

Chapter One - Introduction to Ant Farms

Understanding the Ant Colony

Ants operate within a highly organized society, one that is truly fascinating and mesmerizing to watch within an ant farm.

A family of ants is called a colony. Within the colony are different types of ants, or castes. Each caste of ant has a different and distinct role to play in the colony. Each are essential for the colony to survive.

Ants are highly adaptable and can make an ant nest just about anywhere. Ant nests can be found somewhere as tiny as an acorn seed – or a massive underground network.

The nest is created to provide protection for the ants. The nest also provides the ants with an environment that can accommodate colony growth.

The ant colony is comprised of a queen, workers, soldiers, princesses and drones.

The Queen Ant

An ant colony is a matriarchal society. At its' head is the queen of the colony. There is normally only one queen - but there are exceptions to this where several queens live in the same colony.

The main function of the queen is to lay eggs – this she does on a continuous basis. The queen leaves the colony to mate with drones that are winged (the drones are male ants). This is known as the nuptial flight. After mating, the queen returns to the colony.

After a queen has mated, she is able to lay fertilized eggs on a continuous basis for several years. Throughout her life, the queen will lay millions of eggs.

Some queens can lay thousands of eggs each day.

Amazingly, the queen can determine the sex and status of each egg she lays. For the vast majority of the time, she chooses to lay eggs that will become workers.

She can also create male offspring and future queen ants. These are always winged (or flying ants). This is what allows ants to reproduce. Each year, a new generation of winged ants (males and queens) leave the nest. Their purpose is to mate and found new colonies. They are the new queens and males.

Nanitics

The first generation of ants laid by the queen are known as nanitics. These initial ants are usually significantly smaller than subsequent workers.

This can be explained by the fact that the queen can only provide a restricted amount of food to her growing brood. This compares to subsequent broods who have worker ants foraging for food and bringing it back to the queen and the brood.

Worker Ants

Worker ants are the most numerous within the colony and include all the female ants who are not able to reproduce.

These are the most industrious ants within the colony and perform all the tasks to keep the colony functioning as a unit.

Roles include looking after the queen and the brood; foraging for food; maintaining and expanding the nest; and defending the colony.

Where there is a variation in size amongst the worker ants, these smaller ants would be known as the minor workers.

Soldier Ants

Soldier ants are only present in certain species of ant colonies. The soldier ants are also known as the major workers – or big heads.

In some colonies, there are variations in size amongst the worker ants. Differently sized ants are assigned to distinct castes and perform specific tasks.

Soldier ants are only present in ant species that are 'polymorphic' (refer to section 'Monomorphic and Polymorphic' in Chapter Three).

The soldier ants are female ants that are sterile, like the workers. They are distinct because they are larger and stronger. Their role is to protect the colony from large predators. They also use their strength and large jaws (known as mandibles) to cut and carry large objects.

The harvester ant species have soldier ants that use their strength to crack open hard seeds.

The leaf cutter ant species have soldier ants that work to cut through the thick plants. The minor worker ants then carry the clippings back to the nest.

Some ant species also have median workers. In size, these are in between the minor and major workers.

Winged Princess

The winged princess ants are also referred to as virgin queens. The princess is essentially an unfertilized queen. She has wings and so like the queens and drones, is an alate.

On a warm and humid day, princess ants will leave the nest to mate. This is known as their nuptial flight.

Once she has mated, she will land and seek a suitable nesting place to lay her eggs.

After mating, she has now become a queen. She will usually clip her own wings and will offer them as protein to her offspring.

Winged Drone

The winged drones are the male ants. Like the queens, drones have wings and so are alates – this essentially means that they have wings. These are the only male ants in the colony. They are born from unfertilized eggs.

Chapter One - Introduction to Ant Farms

Due to their wings, the male drones have a very different appearance to the more common worker and soldier ants. The purpose of the wings is so that the drones can mate with the queen mid-air. The drones are usually even smaller than the workers. Their head and mandibles are small.

Mating is the only function that the male ant serves. They are not involved with any of the tasks performed by the worker ants.

Like the princesses, the drones take to the skies on warm and humid days to mate during the nuptial flight.

Once they have mated, the drones die. They live for just a few short months during the mating season.

Chapter Two – Ants Under the Microscope

Ants are invertebrates which means that they do not have a backbone. They have exoskeletons – an external skeleton that makes them both strong and flexible.

The anatomy of an ant can be divided into the external and internal – the outside and the inside.

External Ant Anatomy

As an invertebrate, the ant has its skeleton on the outside. The skeleton of an ant is called a cuticle. It is comprised of many layers (like our skin).

Ant Farms - The Ultimate Formicarium Handbook --Page 22

The skeleton provides the ant with a hard and protective covering (like a suit of armor). It also serves as a strong base for muscle attachment. The ant's skeleton filters out dangerous solar rays. Additionally, the skeleton keeps water vapor inside so that the ant is protected from 'drying out'.

Like all insects, the ant's body is comprised of three sections – the Head, Thorax and Abdomen.

Outside the Head

The outside of the ant's head contains the compound eyes, antennae, mandibles and mouth.

- **Compound Eyes** – Ants have poor vision. They have many small lenses that are placed next to each other which is known as a compound eye. The lenses are called ommatidia. Most adult insects, including ants, have two compound eyes.

  Different species of ants have varying numbers of lenses. For instance, the yellow meadow ant – *Lasius Flavus* – has 45 ommatidia per eye. Compare this to the *Formica cunicularia* which has 460 ommatidia per eye.

Chapter Two – Ants Under the Microscope

Although ants have poor eyesight, their compound eyes enable them to see and detect close movement. Some species of ants are also able to make out general landmarks.

Flying ants have three light sensitive cells on the top of their heads. The purpose of these is to aid them with navigation when flying.

- **Antennae** – These are used to smell, touch, feel and communicate with other ants – the antennae are the most important sensory organ for an ant.

The antennae are attached to the front of the head and can move in front and behind the ant.

As well as its compound eyes, the antennae also help the ant to see. Although the eyes can detect light, when underground many ant species will be able to see nothing at all.

The antennae serve as the principal sense of seeing and hearing. They can sense chemicals in the air, locate scent trails on the ground, and can distinguish changes to air pressure plus notice vibrations.

Because of the importance of the antennae, ants can fold back their antennae across the head. This keeps them protected while in an unsafe situation such as attacking prey or enemy ants.

- **Mandibles / Jaws** – The ants use their mandibles for cutting, holding, fighting and digging. They use them to pick up their brood, food, soil, rubbish, and even each other.

  The ant also uses it mandibles as a means of attack and defense when fighting, for example, against invading ants. They use them to hold onto prey so that they can sting, spray with acid or even tear apart.
  The mandibles are also crucial in building new tunnels and chambers within their colony.
  The jaws are so incredibly strong that some species of ants, such as the leafcutter, can even cut through leather.

  In most species of ants, the jaws have tiny teeth on them. The teeth are larger at the front of the jaw and smaller at the back. This design means they have good grip.

  Amazingly, the mandibles are strong enough to puncture the bodies of their prey – or enemies – but gentle enough to pick up their brood. This is like the jaws and teeth of a lion; strong enough to tear their prey to shreds but also able to tenderly carry around their cubs in their mouths.

- **Mouth -** The ant has smaller mouthparts which it uses to chew food.

The ants have a tongue which they use to taste their food. Unlike humans, it doesn't have muscles in the tongue to move it – it uses blood pressure to make the tongue come out of the mouth. For example, when an ant drinks water, it simply places its tongue on the water. The water travels up the tongue, into the mouth and then down the digestive tract.

The ant also uses its tongue to wash itself. The ant rubs its legs over its body and collects up the dirt. It then passes its front leg over the mouth where the dirt is gathered into a small pocket, the infra-buccal pocket. This is located just below the mouth. When the pocket is full, the ant will empty it into a designated rubbish pile which is usually situated just outside of the nest.

Exterior of the Thorax

All six legs plus wings are attached to the thorax. The thorax is the middle section of the ant's body and is called the mesosoma. The thorax varies depending on the caste of the ant.

Worker ants have a thorax that is rigid whilst the queen ant has a thorax which is flexible – this allows the queen to use the wing muscles.

Along the thorax are spiracles – these are miniscule and invisible to the naked eye. The spiracles are tiny inward facing tubes which enable oxygen to enter the ant's body. Through these same tubes, carbo dioxide is emitted.

- **Legs** – The ant has legs that are equally strong and flexible. The front legs are used to touch objects and to clean its body.

- **Claws** – At the end of each leg are claws. These are used for grasping and gripping onto different surfaces. When the ant is on glass, it will withdraw its' claws and expose a moist pad which is able to cling onto the glass.

External of the Abdomen

Abdomen – The abdomen is comprised of the gaster and stinger.

- **Gaster** – The gaster houses vital organs. It is made up of seven segments that gives great capacity for flexibility.
- **Stinger** – Whilst not all ant species have a stinger, they can still spray acid into wounds. Those that do have a stinger use it to inject formic acid into their victims.

Internal Ant Anatomy

Now that you know understand the outside of the ant's anatomy, it is time to explore what's on the inside.

- **Brain** – The brain can store simple information and processes sensory data that it receives from the antennae, joints, body hairs and eyes. This is how the ant is able to understand its surroundings and react to its environment.

- **Heart** – The heart of an ant is shaped like a tube, completely different to the heart of humans and all other mammals. An ant's heart is more similar to one of our veins - it runs throughout the ant's entire body, surrounding all the internal organs with blood. The blood of an ant is a clear / yellowish liquid.

- **Nerve Cord** – This helps to coordinate movement by sending electronic message through the ant's body – via the nerve cord.

- **Crop** – The ant uses the crop to store 'social' food that is to be shared with the other ants in the colony.

- **Stomach** – This is where the ant digests its own food using acids.

- **Rectum** – Waste products are held in the rectum. All waste is left in a nominated waste area which is located outside of the nest.

- **The Sting** – Also known as poison glands or formic acid duct. This is where formic acid is contained. Formic acid is used as the ant's weapon to attack or defend. The formic acid is either injected into or sprayed onto the ant's victim.

- **Dufour's Gland –** This is where the ant produces chemicals known as pheromones. These are used to communicate with other ants – to alert other ants, to guide them (perhaps to a source of food) or to attract mates. The purpose of the Dufour's gland is to secrete chemicals.

Chapter Three – Exploring Ant Behavior

The Nuptial Flight

The nuptial flight marks the true beginning stage of the life cycle of an ant.

This is where the reproductive, flying alate ants take to the skies. This includes both the princesses and drones.

The alates fly away from their nest. This avoids inbreeding.

When the princesses are ready to mate, they release pheromones. These attract the drones. The princesses frequently try to outfly the drones. This guarantees that the princess mates with a drone that is strong. Mating occurs in mid-air – during the nuptial flight.

Princesses usually mate with several drones. They store the sperm in their 'sperm pocket'. The sperm will be used to fertilize tens of millions of eggs and will last throughout the lifetime of princess.

Subsequent to mating, the drones die relatively quickly. The princess lands in search for a safe place to build her nest. She has now become a queen.

Life Cycle of the Ant

There are four stages to the ant' life cycle – egg, larvae, pupae (or for some species cocoon) and adult. It takes approximately 8 to 12 weeks for the eggs to become adult ants. However, the time varies considerably depending on surrounding temperature, humidity levels, plus quantity and type of food available.

The eggs, larvae and pupae are all known as the 'brood' of the ant colony. The brood are tended to by the worker ants.

The ant life cycle is a form of metamorphosis. It is the same process that a caterpillar uses to transform into a butterfly.

In mature colonies, the brood are moved around the nest. This ensures that the brood is kept at optimum growing temperatures.

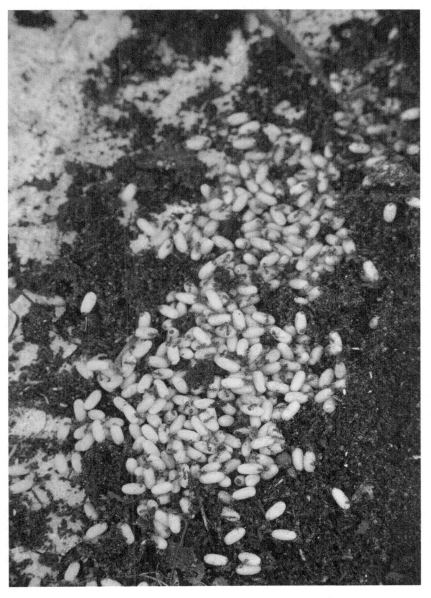

Eggs – Ant eggs are microscopic – just 0.5mm in diameter and weighing approximately 0.0005g. Eggs are shaped like a kidney. They have a smooth sticky outer layer which makes them bond together in a mass. This enables adult ants to move the eggs about in a bundle. This way, the eggs can be moved quickly in the face of danger.

The eggs are usually visible in an ant farm. Look for clusters of tiny white dots – these are the eggs!

Larvae – After about 7 – 14 days the larvae will begin to appear from the eggs. The eggs look like minute maggots.

As the larvae grows, skin is shed. This happens about 3 times in total. With each molt, the larvae will increase in size – from 1mm to 4mm. They also become increasingly hairy with each molt. Some of these hairs hook onto the hairs of other larvae – just like when eggs, by hooking together, the larvae can be transported together as a bundle by the adult ants.

Even though the larvae have no legs, they are able to make small movements. For example, they can bend their head towards a source of food – or even move very slowly if necessary.

Adult worker ants bring food to the larvae. They either suck up the juices of solid foods brought to them or they consume regurgitated food from the worker ants.

Pupae / Cocoon – Once the larvae have experienced all of their skin molts, they change into the final stage – the pupae. This occurs after about 24 to 27 days.

Pupae have the appearance of white waxy ants. They have their legs and antennae folded up against their bodies.

Some ant species, such as the Lasius Niger, do not have a pupa stage. Instead, the larvae spin themselves into a cocoon from which it will transform into an adult ant.

Adult Ant – Following a further 13 to 28 days, the adult ant will emerge with a pale and soft appearance. After just a few hours, the ant will darken in color and its' exoskeleton will become hard.

The only observable difference between young ants and an older worker is a variation in color – the younger ants will be pale with a yellow hue. Once the exoskeleton is fully hardened, these young ants will become black - it will then be impossible to differentiate between the younger ants and older ones.

How Ants Communicate

Ants communicate very effectively with each other, but not through sound or sight.

Chapter Three – Exploring Ant Behavior

Ants are naturally programmed to follow rules and signals that they receive through chemical smells (pheromones), vibrations and touch.

This incredible system allows all ants in the colony to live in perfect harmony. Every single ant within the colony is working with exactly the same purpose – survival of the colony.

Pheromones are scented chemicals produced by the ants. They are released from glands found all over their body. The pheromones enable the ants to communicate with all the other ants within the colony.

Ants use the tips of their hyper sensitive antennae to detect pheromones. The left and right antennae can direct the ant which way to turn with the varying pheromone strength. Ants rely on their antennae for communication. An ant that has missing or damaged antennae will be very confused, disorganized, and disoriented.

Ants use approximately ten to twenty different pheromone scents. The number varies depending on the species of ant. Each scent communicates a 'chemical word' that is understood by the whole colony.

Pheromones can be used to send for other ants. Depending on the nature of the pheromone, a few ants will be called – or thousands of ants. This will depend on what the ant needs – attacking prey, defending the colony, locating a sweet source of food, or the relocation of the colony.

Ants also use pheromones to alert other ants to danger. Indeed, when an ant is squashed, it emits a specific pheromone.

Pheromones are also used by ants to differentiate between ants of the same colony and ants belonging to a different colony.

The queen ant has her own unique pheromones that allow other ants to know of her status – and can communicate whether the worker ants need to begin raising new princesses and drones.

Defense Systems

Ants attack and defend themselves by biting and in many species, by stinging. This can be either injecting or spraying their victim with chemicals. Some species use formic acid and others a variety of protein components.

Although not fatal to humans, the bullet ant (indigenous to Central and South America), is considered to have the most painful sting of any insect. The jack jumper ants have a sting that can be fatal – an antivenom has been developed in response. Fire ants have a venom sac which holds piperidine alkaloids. Their stings are very painful and can be dangerous to some people.

Trap jaw ants have remarkably large mandibles that can lock back at 180 degrees. The mandibles can snap shut on prey or objects – this is in response to touch on the sensory hairs that are located on the inside of their mandibles. This operates in a similar way to the Venus fly trap.

The mandibles of the trap jaw ant can exert forces 300 times its own weight, at speeds of around 230 km/h or 140 mph. They can be used to kill or injure prey – or in response to danger, it can push its head to the ground, and fling itself away.

Protecting against Pathogens

As well as defending the colony against predators, the ants also need to defend the colony against pathogens.

Some worker ants are responsible for maintaining the hygiene of the colony. This involves disposing of dead ants in the nest. Chemical scents are released from the dead ants which is what triggers the behavior by the worker ants.

Ants defend their colonies against physical threats such as overheating and flooding using elaborate nest architecture. For example, one species of ants that live within plant hollows, respond to flooding by drinking water inside the nest and excreting it outside.

Foraging for Food

Ants have established complex and varied ways to find, forage, distribute and in some ways, to make their own food.

Ants consume more than any other animal species. It is thought that ants eat more meat than lions, wolves and tigers combined!

Chapter Three – Exploring Ant Behavior

In agriculture, ants can be considered as pests as they are able to devour crops extraordinarily rapidly.

With an incredibly varied diet, ants feed on an enormous range of foods – from engine oil to other ant species.

The majority of ant species are omnivores. Their diet includes seeds, nectar and other invertebrates.

Army ants are carnivores. They hunt, kill and eat prey including worms, spiders and sometimes small vertebrates like lizards.

Leaf cutting ants are herbivores. They consume a type of fungus – they grow this from the chewed up remains of leaves and flowers that they take back to their nests.

Joining Forces

Numerous species of ants join forces with other invertebrates and plants to find food.

For example, some ants herd together sap feeding insects 'homopterans', such as aphids, scale bugs and mealy bugs. This is essentially farming on the part of the ants.

The sap feeding insects extract food from plants and pass some of it onto the ants. This is a highly nutritious nectar / honeydew for the ants. To make it a symbiotic relationship, the ants look after these insects and protect them - in return for the nectar.

Some species of ants can stroke the back of aphids with their antennae. This produces a honeydew droplet.

The ants sometimes move the insects to areas on the plants with the best sap.

During rainfall, ants have been known to move the insects to a more sheltered location – sometimes even their own nest.

Although this appears to be a reciprocal arrangement, research has revealed that the ants seem to have the upper hand. In some circumstances, the ants have clipped the wings off the aphids to prevent them flying away. They have also been known to use chemicals to stop the insects from flying away – essentially drugging them.

Sharing Food with the Colony

Ants share their food with other ants within the nest. Worker ants leave the nest to forage for food. They then store some liquid food in their 'social stomach' or crop.

The worker ants will then regurgitate the food and share it amongst the other ants in the colony. This process of sharing liquid foods is called trophallaxis.

Trophallaxis is utilized as a further means of communication. It is likely to help spread the odor so that ants can recognize and identify ants from within the same nest.

How Ants Learn

Imitation is perhaps the most common way that animals learn behaviors. In a similar way to mammals, ants have been observed to be involved in interactive teaching.

Some species of ants, such as temnothorax albipennis, have been seen teaching other ants. For example, an experienced forager will go foraging for food with a nest mate who is new to foraging. The experienced forager ant is essentially teaching the new ant. She responds to the younger ant, slowing down when the ant behind starts to lag, and speeding up again when the ant behind catches up.

Controlled experiments have also taken place that reveal that individual ants tend to choose their role within the nest in accordance to their previous experience.

For example, a group of cerapachys biroi ants were divided into two. The success or otherwise of foraging was controlled. One group was always rewarded with plenty of food and prey. In contrast, the other group were always unsuccessful, finding no food or prey.

This led to the successful group being even more adventurous with their foraging efforts. In comparison, the unsuccessful group of ants came out to forage less and less.

One month later, the successful foragers continued in their foraging role whilst the unsuccessful group of ants had moved within the nest, caring for the queen and brood.

Monomorphic and Polymorphic Ant Colonies

You will notice that in some species of ants, the workers are all the same size. This compares to other colonies where the workers vary in size. In a monomorphic species, all the worker ants are the same size. In a polymorphic species, there are varying sizes of ants.

This can be connected to evolution. Over time, colonies have become bigger and more complex. It is considered that the increase in size and complexity created a need for more specialized tasks within the colony. This led to the evolution and development of the worker caste.

Within the worker castes, labor is divided into different tasks.

It is generally thought that ants with a monomorphic worker caste are not as highly evolved as those with a polymorphic worker caste.

In the monomorphic species, the job of the worker ant changes as the ant becomes older. This compares to polymorphic species where different workers are assigned to specific tasks – this is then reflected in varying sizes of the worker ants.

In a polymorphic colony, the smaller worker ants would be known as the minor workers. Some would be responsible for meeting the needs of the queen and her brood; others would be foragers and bring back food to share with the colony; others would oversee nest maintenance and expansion.

A polymorphic colony would also include major workers, also known as soldier ants. These are unreproductive female ants. They are larger and stronger than the other worker ants. Their role is to protect the colony from predators. They use their strength and large mandibles (jaws) to cut or carry large objects.

Some ant species also have median workers. These are sized between the minor and major workers.

Chapter Four – Getting Ready for your Ant Farm

Starting Out

Most ant keepers prefer to begin their own colony from a single queen ant. This means locating or buying a newly mated queen – she will be the source of your colony and it will be able to thrive for several years.

However, building up an ant colony like this is a lengthy process. Indeed, if the colony starts with a single queen, you will be waiting for a couple of months to see a small colony of workers. It will take about a year for the colony to develop into a large, established colony of about 100 ants.

This approach is not suited to everyone. Children especially may prefer a quicker process with less of a long-term commitment.

Digging up a wild colony might be a better option, especially for children. You will have many workers instantly. And if your child does lose interest, at least you can release the colony back into the wild again.

If you decide to collect an already established wild colony, note that you may well find your nest short of a queen. Indeed, the queen ant can be very difficult to locate and identify. There is also the risk that the wild ants will not adapt easily to their change of home and habitat.

Before you are ready to obtain an ant colony or queen, you need to ensure that you are ready and prepared. Let's think about what you need.

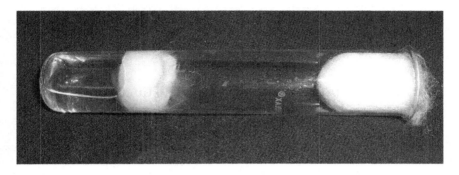

By Garinger - Own work, CC BY-SA 2.5,
https://commons.wikimedia.org/w/index.php?curid=2031142

Basic Ant Necessities

Starter kits are available, and you can purchase ant farms in a variety of sizes, shapes and designs. Many ant keepers choose to make / build their own formicarium. Basic equipment that you will need includes the following;

- Formicarium, also known as ant farm. This is what you will keep the ants in. The formicarium is like an aquarium but is specifically for ants.
- Test Tube
- Cotton Balls

- Small container
- Vaseline
- Or - Unperfumed talcum powder
- Alcohol (70% will be adequate)
- Ant food

The Formicarium

The formicarium is comprised of two distinct parts – the nest and an area for foraging (like an outdoor compartment).

Reflecting the huge variation of ant nest sizes in the wild, ants thrive in all sizes of formicarium. It is not necessary to have numerous nest chambers and tubes with a huge area for foraging. Remember that ants are such tiny creatures – they do not require a great deal of space.

The nest area will contain many tunnels and will be covered by a glass slate. This is so that you can observe the ants within the nest. The glass is covered by something so that the nest is kept in the dark, imitating a natural ant nest. The foraging area replicates the area outside of a wild nest. This is where you will place food for the ants that they will find and bring back to the nest. It is also the area where they will leave their rubbish – that you will need to clear away to keep the formicarium clean and thriving.

Chapter Four – Getting Ready for your Ant Farm

Beginning with a Test Tube

A test tube is an excellent starting formicarium for your new colony. It is the best possible start when you are introducing a single queen and waiting for the colony to emerge.

In addition to being cheap, it provides the perfect conditions for an ant colony and enables you to have clear and easy visibility of the ants. The queen ant will stay within the test tube for a few weeks or months, until her initial set of workers appear.

By Messor structor - Own work, CC BY-SA 3.0,
https://commons.wikimedia.org/w/index.php?curid=2136683

Avoid providing a small colony with a big formicarium at the beginning. A formicarium that is too large for the colony will not thrive. This results in the ants dumping their waste in an empty section of their nest – somewhere that you are unable to reach to remove it. Inevitably, the waste will go moldy and turn to rot – this will be the ruin of your ant colony.

If the nest is the correct size according to the size of the colony, the ants will keep their nest clean themselves.

Queen ants tend to thrive in a test tube environment. This is likely because the test tube arrangement imitates an underground chamber for a recently mated queen. This usually means that she will start laying eggs to begin her ant colony.

When your colony outgrows the test tube, you will be ready to move the queen, brood and worker ants to a larger formicarium.

Ant keepers tend to wait until the queen ant has several worker ants before transferring them into a formicarium. This is because the queen needs a team of worker ants to assist her with moving the brood, tending to the brood and to look after the nest.

Some ant keepers wait until she has around ten to twenty workers before making the transfer to the formicarium. Other ant keepers prefer to wait until the test tube is completely full of ants. Both approaches work well – most important is to wait till the queen has the support of a group of worker ants.

Test Tube Nest Set-Up

Before setting up your test tube nest, ensure that your hands are clean. This will avoid the unnecessary spread of germs into the new ant nest.

Fill the lower half of the test tube with clean water. Some ant keepers prefer to use bottled water. Take a clean cotton ball and push down to half way. Use a clean cotton swab to push down the cotton ball. If the cotton ball is too large, you may need to tear a piece off. Make sure you press down the cotton ball into the tube quickly – this will help to avoid air bubbles.

Push the cotton ball so that it is just immersed in water. When in position (about half way in the tube), push gently several times so that the entire cotton ball becomes moist.

The test tube set up works well as the queen and her ants can decide whether to stay within the humid area next to the cotton ball or in the dry area (near the top of the test tube).

When you have placed the queen ant inside the test tube, use a dry cotton ball to seal the end of the tube.

At this time, there is no need to provide the ants with additional water. This is because they have water available in their test tube.

The queen is likely to lay her first set of eggs within one to three days and she is likely to stay in the test tube set up for approximately one month. It is beneficial to keep the test tube in a dark area to closer imitate an underground chamber.

Some ant keepers cover the test tube in tinfoil to make it dark for the ants, simulating a natural ant nest.

You can close the end of the test tube off with another cotton ball. This will create a seal to prevent your ants from escaping plus allow some air to circulate through the test tube.

Chapter Four – Getting Ready for your Ant Farm

If you prefer, you can use a test tube cap – but place a small piece of cotton or paper towel inside when you close the lid – this will allow air to flow in. Alternatively, poke holes in the cap with a pin. Ants do not require a lot of oxygen, but they will eventually die in a container that is completely sealed.

Chapter Five – Sourcing Your Ants

Ways to Source Ants

Ant keepers employ a variety of methods as ways to source their ants. There are several different ways to obtain ants for an ant farm – this will be affected by when you want to start the colony and how long you would hope your ant farm to last for.

You can purchase ants through online retailers and pet stores. However, ants available commercially like this do not include a queen ant. You can sustain an ant farm with only worker ants for several months.

Another way to begin an ant farm is to collect your own worker ants from your own backyard or local area.

The US governs that it is illegal to ship live queen ants across state border lines. Consequently, ants sold contain no queens. This prevents the introduction of non-native ant species. This is to avoid ants that can reproduce entering other states and starting colonies that could damage agriculture or have a negative impact on the ecosystem.

This contrasts to Europe where there are no laws dictating owning, keeping, buying or selling non-protected species.

Chapter Five – Sourcing Your Ants

There are only laws controlling ant species that are protected such as *Formica rufa*.

However, the queen ant is what makes things so enthralling – so that you can see how the colony operates together – and watch it expand with the growing brood. By starting with a queen, you will soon have a thriving colony of ants.

The AntsCanada Global Ant Nursery Project was founded to help potential ant keepers start a colony with a queen. They will help you to locate ant sellers in your area to buy ants from. This means that ant enthusiasts can enjoy keeping local ant species. It avoids the problem of shipping and crossing state lines.

One of the most popular ways to source ants amongst ant keepers is to go out and find your own queen (in your local area) that you bring back to your ant farm. This is an excellent method and thoroughly rewarding – you will essentially be catching the pure source which will be able to sustain your colony for many years.

You can try and collect a colony with queen that is already established in the wild. However, it can be difficult to identify the queen.

Additionally, there is a risk that the whole colony may not be able to adjust to their new home. A newly mated queen is much more receptive and able to adapt to a new home.

Purchasing Ants

The easiest way to start your ant farm is to buy ants either online or through a pet store. The most common species available tends to be red harvester ants. Queen ants cannot be purchased due to USDA restrictions (see previous section 'Ways to Source Ants').

The ants will be delivered to you in a tube. They will need to be transferred to your formicarium on arrival so ensure that you have everything ready in preparation.

Purchased farm ants tend to live between 3 to 6 months. Some may even live as long as 8 months.

If you have sand in your formicarium, you will be able to use the same sand for two colonies of ants. Simply remove the sand and sift out any dead ants remaining from the original batch and remove any old food.

Collecting Worker Ants

The fastest and easiest option of sourcing ants is to collect some worker ants, without a queen.

Necessary equipment for collecting ants includes;

- a small hand shovel to dig and scoop up ants.

- container to store the ants in. A plastic food storage container or glass jar would be very suitable to store the ants in and transport them back home. Make sure that you can close the lid tightly to prevent the ants from making an escape.

To collect ants, you will need to locate a thriving ant colony. Start by exploring your yard and if unsuccessful, check out local wooded areas.

Spring and summer are the optimum time to collect ants. At this time, the ants are busy and consequently, easier to find. It is difficult to find many ants during the winter – in the cold, ants are quite inactive and unable to move very quickly. Additionally, many ants in temperate zones, will actually be hibernating.

Use caution when collecting wild ants. Note that some kinds of ants will sting to protect their colonies. These types of ants are probably best avoided. Research the types of ants that populate your area and make sure you know what ants you are looking for – and, just as importantly, if there are any kinds of ants to avoid.

Ant colonies are most likely to be found in soil, in small mounds close to the ground, underneath rocks, in pieces of wood or even in acorns. The ants found on the ground are probably the easiest ants to collect.

Once you have found an ant colony, you will need to dig your way into it using the hand shovel. If you find your colony set within soil or in a dirt mound, simply dig about six inches into the entrance of the colony.

If you find a colony hidden underneath a rock or similar, simply overturn to reveal the ants.

Simply scoop up the ants and place into your container.

Be sure to return everything to how you found it afterwards – for example return rocks to their original position. This ensures that the habitat is only minimally disturbed and other organisms may still use it.

Like purchasing ants, the problem with collecting worker ants is that they will soon dwindle away with the absence of their queen.

Capturing your own Queen Ant

Capturing your own queen ant requires patience and can only be done at a very specific time of the year. However, this way you will be able to witness the very beginning of the ant colony life cycle which is undoubtedly very exciting and fascinating. Moreover, the queen will keep your colony sustained with a perpetual life cycle of worker ants.

GFDL 1.2, https://commons.wikimedia.org/w/index.php?curid=1512438

Chapter Five – Sourcing Your Ants

To have a chance of capturing a queen ant, you need to wait till the right time of the year – when she is involved in her nuptial flight. It must be during the few weeks of the year when mating occurs. Every species of ant has its nuptial flight at a set time in the year.

During the nuptial flight, the young winged queens and drones (male ants) take flight. They mate while in the air and finally land back to ground several hours later. The queen will usually mate with several males. While the males die after mating, the mated females break off their wings.

The queen's next step will be to find a new location to begin her own colony. Once established in her new nest, the queen will give birth to her first set of babies – who will become her worker ants.

Be aware that it is challenging to find a queen ant. It is helpful if you can find out what time of the year and what time of the day mating tends to occur in your local area. Regardless, you will need to be patient. Depending on the species of ant and where they live, the nuptial flight is affected by day length, temperature and rainfall.

The only time you will be able to capture a queen is during the nuptial flight or immediately afterwards - when she is searching for a new nest location. After this point, the queens spend the rest of their lives in their underground nests.

Chapter Five – Sourcing Your Ants

Some ant species tend to start new nests in the springtime while others wait till after the summer monsoon rains. It depends on the temperature and the ant species.

Many queen ants tend to take flight following a summer rain. The rain appears to stimulate their mating period.

Also consider that you are most likely to find a queen ant in an area where there are a lot of ant colonies present.

Queens that have just mated will be looking for the right place to build their new nest. Some newly mated queens will have their wings attached. However, most will tear them off quickly as they start to look for a suitable new home. This is because the wings make the queen easier to spot by predators.

You will be able to spot the queens on the ground as they are much larger than the worker ants. You should also be able to see two scars on their thorax – this is where their wings used to be attached.

The ordinary worker ants that you commonly see crawling on the ground will not be able to help – these ants cannot reproduce so your colony cannot be sustained.

If you happen to spot a queen on the ground, you should be able to gently pick her up in your fingers – being very careful and gentle. During the time of nuptial flights, it is a great idea to take some bottles or containers with you – you never know when you might be lucky enough to spot your queen ant.

Collect as many queen ants as you can find – not every queen will successfully start up a new colony.

It is also possible to capture a queen who is just starting to build a nest. Indeed, they won't be very deep within the ground. Use a shovel to carefully take a look. You will be able to identify a nest in the making – look for a small hole in the ground that is surrounded by a small heap of fresh dirt.

If you begin to dig in a hole that does contain a queen, she is likely to emerge from the dirt in an attempt to escape.

Whether you are successful in your search or otherwise, be sure to refill any holes that you dig.

Identifying Queen Ants that have Mated

It is frequently assumed that a queen who has broken off her wings has mated. This is not necessarily the case – ant keepers find that some queens who have broken off their wings never go on to lay eggs.

Likewise, a queen who still has her wings attached may still have mated. Queens with wings attached have been known to lay eggs.

The only guarantee that your queen is fertilized is when the first eggs are laid – and you begin to see the worker ants emerge.

One indication of fertilization is if the queen's abdomen (known as her gaster) looks bloated. This tends to occur several days or weeks after mating. Another sign is if the queen begins to frequently clean the tip of her gaster.

Global Ant Nursery Project

If you lack the time to go out searching for your queen ant – or if you are unsuccessful in your attempts to do so, it is possible to adopt an ant colony that has been farmed from a queen in your local area.

The Global Ant Nursery Project is a worldwide network of AntsCanada-recruited expert ant farmers. These ant farmers are known as GAN farmers – they raise and sell local ant colonies complete with a queen to people within their region.

Chapter Six – History of Ant Farms and their Rise in Popularity

Ant keeping has increased in popularity over the last sixty years. The trend first began in the 1960's although the first formicarium was invented and designed at the beginning of the twentieth century in the 1900's.

Charles Janet

The very first formicarium was invented and exhibited by Charles Janet in the 1900's. Janet was a French engineer, company director, inventor and biologist. He is possibly best known for his work on the periodic table.

Janet was a prolific inventor and created much of his own equipment. As part of his study on ants, Janet invented the formicarium. The purpose was simply to make the ant colony visible – being enclosed by two panes of glass. He did not intend to bring the formicarium to market, but utilized it in his own research.

Frank Eugene Austin

It wasn't until Frank Eugene Austin that the first

formicarium became commercially available. This was introduced in around 1929. Austin had his formicarium patented. He tended to include paintings or wooden scenes of palaces above the ground level.

Austin was an inventor and professor at Dartmouth College (Thayer School of Engineering). He did not refer to his formicarium as an ant farm but as an "educational apparatus" or "scenic insect cage". In a magazine article that featured Austin's invention, it was referred to as an "ant palace".

Milton Levine

Milton Levine was the founder of Uncle Milton Industries – still trading and manufacturing in science and nature toys today. Uncle Milton industries bought 'ant farms' to the market, making them commercially available to all ant enthusiasts.

In 1956, Levine created and designed his own version of a formicarium. He states that this was independent of the inventions by Austin.

Even as a young child, Levine had been captivated by ants – he would collect ants in jars. In 1956, he became inspired at a Fourth of July picnic where he observed a colony of ants. He decided that if he and lots of children were fascinated by ants then "we should make an antarium".

This was when the idea of the 'ant farm' was born. Levine worked with his brother in law, Joe Cossman – an enthusiastic entrepreneur, to bring ant farms to the popular market.

The ant farms were originally sold for $1.29 – and consisted of a six by nine-inch container and a box of sand.

After purchasing the ant farm, customers could request a shipment of 25 ants. The species of ants used were Pogonomyrmex californicus – a species native to southwestern USA.

The success and popularity of Levine's ant farms was quite phenomenal. By 2011, at the time of his death, over 200 million units had sold, with a growth rate of 30,000 a month.

Ant farms are now widely available and are still increasing in popularity with adults and children alike.

Ant Farms Today

Today, there are several types of ant farms available both in stores and online. The majority of these, especially those designed for children, are intended for an ant colony without a queen.

These are suitable as a short-term project but cannot be sustained, like a full colony with a queen. The ant farms are perfect for younger children who will be able to observe some aspects of ant behavior.

Sand Based Ant Farms

Traditional ant farms were filled with sand and this remains a popular choice today.

By The original uploader was Jonespapa at Hungarian Wikipedia - Transferred from hu.wikipedia to Commons., CC BY-SA 3.0, https://commons.wikimedia.org/w/index.php?curid=2994683

Where an ant farm is filled with sand, it is important to avoid moving it as much as possible. This is because once your ants have started tunneling, there is a risk that movement will cause the tunnels to cave in and smother the ants.

Traditional sand based ant farms come with a bag of sand that you can simply pour into the ant habitat. The ants will do the rest of the work! The same sand can be used with two batches of ants – sand refill packs are available for future batches of ants.

Gel Based Ant Farms

Modern ant farms are filled with a space age gel. This type of ant habitat emerged after a NASA experiment which looked to see if ants could survive in zero gravity.

The gel based ant farms have become incredibly popular and are the most prevalent on the market today.

The gel means that there is much less daily maintenance and is ideal for people unable to commit to regular and daily care.

The gel is nutrient rich and is designed to enable the ants to thrive without the need for additional food or water. Ant gel is made from seaweed extracts, rich in water, amino acids and sugars. The gel also has a fungicide which will prevent rotting, even with the high moisture levels within the ant farm.

The gel based ant farms come already filled with the space age gel. It is ready for use immediately.

You may notice that your ants do not eat or tunnel in the gel for the first few days. This is because the gel substance is completely new to them – they do not always realize straight away that they can eat the gel and create tunnels within it.

The majority of these farms come with a tool so that you can start the tunnel building. Your ants may continue to build the tunnel that you start – or they may follow your example but create their own new tunnels. Either way is perfect.

The gel ant farms work well for people with a passing interest in ants. Indeed, they are ideal for children who first show an interest in ant keeping. However, there are some serious disadvantages and they are not suitable for a colony that you plan to sustain.

The gel will eventually dry up and become hard. It can also become tacky, especially in the center – consequently the gel can sometimes stick onto the ants.

Chapter Six – History of Ant Farms and their Rise in Popularity

The gel ant farms are only suitable for ant colonies without a queen as they have a limited life span. Many experienced ant keepers view the gel farms as unsuitable for long-term serious ant keeping. Some regard them as acceptable for short-term use and observation whilst others would say they should not be used.

Regardless, the gel ant farms have undoubtedly bought ant farming into widespread popularity and awareness. They may well serve as an introduction for many people before venturing into more serious ant keeping.

Chapter Seven – Introducing the Ants

Here Comes the Queen

You have your artificial nest ready and waiting (the test tube with water reservoir) – and you can now add in your fertilized queen.

The test tube set-up is designed so that the queen will not need any food until the first workers arrive. Before then, the queen will survive on her stored fats and proteins. She has adequate nutrients to raise her first generation of worker ants. Refer to following section on fully-claustral and semi-claustral queens.

By Eveha - Own work, CC BY-SA 4.0,
https://commons.wikimedia.org/w/index.php?curid=36775450

The ideal beginning for the queen is to be somewhere dark where she will not be disturbed – such as a cupboard or drawer. Otherwise, cover the test tube with aluminum foil. Check on the queen once a week but disturb her as little as possible.

Most important in the first few days or even weeks is to avoid any kind of disturbance to the queen.

Once the workers have arrived, you can take her out of the dark.

When using the test tube nest set up, there is no need to add water as this will be available within the test tube.

Differences Among Queens

There are essentially three different types of queen ants; fully-claustral, semi-claustral, and socially parasitic.

Each of these different types of queens have different needs and feeding requirements. Feeding the queen (or not) depends on which type you have.

Fully-Claustral

It is not necessary to offer food or extra nourishment to a fully-claustral queen. They can survive without food for several months because they are nourished through their fat and food stores.

Despite this, some ant keepers choose to offer food for extra nourishment.

The only problem is that the queen can experience stress at any minor disturbance – including offering food. If the queen does become stressed, she can delay laying eggs or can even eat her existing brood.

The fully-claustral queens tend to prefer sweet foods as opposed to proteins (such as insects). There will always be exceptions to this however. Ordinarily, a droplet of sugar water, a dab of honey or maple syrup will be perfectly adequate. You could consider adding whey protein shake powder into any sweet mixture that you offer. This will be an additional and valuable source of protein.

Be sure to keep all your movements slow and gradual to reduce the amount of disturbance caused to the queen.

The fully-claustral queens are usually larger than semi-claustral queens, with smaller heads in proportion to their bodies (compared to semi-claustral and social parasitic).

Since they spend their entire time in the nest during the founding stage, they do not need to forage.

Semi-Claustral

Semi-claustral queen ants do require feeding. You can still raise them in the typical test tube set up. Simply leave the test tube open – there is no need to create a seal with the second cotton wool ball. Place the test tube within a container.

Add the food to the container. The queen will come out of the test tube, find and carry back the food to her test tube nest.

The semi-claustral queens tend to accept both protein and sugar. For protein, a small insect will be sufficient every 2 to 3 days.

When giving sugar, you only need to give a tiny droplet – it is better that she consumes it all so that it is not left to rot inside the nest. You could also consider placing the sugar droplet on a small piece of tinfoil (that fits inside the test tube) – this may help to keep the nest area clean and prevent it from becoming sticky.

Semi-claustral queens are generally thinner than fully-claustral.

Although more difficult to maintain, these queens are fascinating to watch.

Social Parasites

The third type of queen ant is a social parasite. These queens are usually bulky, like the fully-claustral queen. However, they have larger heads and mandibles in proportion to their body (compared to fully claustral queens).

These queens need a host to establish their colony. In the natural world, they would invade a colony of their preferred host species, kill the queen and use the workforce to raise her own brood.

To care for a socially parasitic queen, you will need to find out the preferred host species – collect some of these workers and brood and then attempt to introduce them. Be aware that some social parasite colonies rely on 'slaves'. Indeed, some of these ant species have evolved to the point that they are reliant on recruiting slaves from other colonies. This makes raising a socially parasitic species in a formicarium more challenging.

Waiting for Eggs

Many queen ants will begin to lay eggs just a few short
hours after being housed within the artificial nest.
However, it is not uncommon for the queen to take a few
days and sometimes even a few weeks.

If your queen has not laid any eggs, it could be because it is
near the hibernation time of the year. This is especially true
if you have captured the queen September onwards –
before laying her eggs, your queen may decide to hibernate.

Once she comes out of hibernation, she will then lay her
first batch of ant eggs. Never give up on your queen – be
very patient!

Ant Farms - The Ultimate Formicarium Handbook --Page 76

Simply provide the queen with a safe place where it is dark. Only check on her once a week to keep disturbances to an absolute minimum.

Worker ants will take approximate 4 to 6 weeks to emerge from the eggs. This process is usually quicker where the nest is warm. The arrival of the worker ants means that you can now take the queen out of the dark.

Nanitic Worker Ants

The first worker ants to emerge are called the nanitics. These ants are usually substantially smaller than the subsequent worker ants. This is because the queen is only able to provide a limited amount of food compared to that which the foraging ants can provide.

Once these initial worker ants mature, they will be desperate to leave the test tube nest and forage.

You will notice that they start to try and open the nest – tearing at the cotton plug. Before this point, the queen will have been providing them with nourishment. Now it is time that you need the provide them with food.

Chapter Eight – Caring for an Fledgling Colony

Feeding the Workers

Once the worker ants have become established, they will forage for their own food - for themselves, their queen and the brood. At the beginning though, they will need a little help.

At first, feed the worker ants directly into the test tube. Consider placing the food on a small piece of tinfoil which you can carefully slide into the test tube. The tinfoil helps to keep the test tube clean – when they have finished, simply remove it.

The ants need two main nutrients – sugar and protein (amino acids).

Sugar is needed as an energy source, mainly for the worker ants. Most ants are unable to consume solid food, so sugar must be given in a liquid form.

Suitable sources of sugar include;

- Sugar water (also known as sugar solution)
- Honey Solution
- Fruit (such as apples, oranges, grapes)
- Honeydew surrogate

The colony needs protein for the queen to produce eggs and for the larvae to grow.

Suitable sources of protein include;

- Insects (such as fruit flies, crickets, cockroaches, other arthropods like spiders)
- Eggs, meat
- Free amino acids, protein whey
- Honeydew surrogate

Most ant keepers tend to offer a mixture of sugar water and insects.

Sugar Water

To make sugar water for ants, simply mix 7 units of water with 1 unit of sugar. This is the same technique for making honey water.

Honeydew Surrogate

Honeydew surrogate is a solution of sugars and amino acids. It was invented by Dutch ant keepers on AntForum.nl. It is designed to simulate honeydew – this is

Chapter Eight – Caring for an Fledgling Colony

the sugary liquid that is excreted by aphids – and is the main natural sugar source for numerous species of ants.

Homemade honeydew surrogate contains sugars, amino acids plus vitamins. The sugar and vitamins are in similar concentrations to that of natural honeydew – but the amino acid is ten times higher than that of actual organic honeydew.

This is deliberate – because in the natural environment ants would be travelling much greater distances to locate and collect honeydew (compared to ants within a formicarium). Therefore, ants in the wild will be using up a significant part of the sugars in their travels – consequently concentrating the amino acids in honeydew by the time they return to their nest.

Honeydew surrogate tends to be very popular among many different species of ants. The amino acids present in the honeydew surrogate are an excellent alternative to insect protein. However, insects should also be provided to guarantee that the ants are provided with sufficient supplies and a varied range of protein sources.

Honeydew surrogate is easy to prepare, and it is inexpensive. It will also last for quite a while.

Recipe for Honeydew Surrogate;

- 25ml liquid amino acids
- 50ml maple syrup or honey

- 130gms glucose (or table / granulated sugar)
- 480ml water

Liquid amino acids are available to buy in sport supplement stores. The only problem is that you will only need one ampoule and they are normally sold in packs of 10, 20 or 30. It may be that you can share the ampoules with other ant keepers – or try to buy one from a local gym (or body builder).

Method;

- Dissolve the glucose in the water (use a large container). Stir or heat to allow the glucose to dissolve.
- Add the maple syrup (or honey if using) and stir thoroughly
- Add the liquid amino acid and stir
- Ready!

This recipe will make around 650ml honeydew surrogate so will last a while. Freeze all the honeydew surrogate that you don't need to use straight away.

If you have some syringes, this is an excellent way to freeze and then defrost the solution when you are ready to use it. Simply remove the syringe from the freezer and allow to thaw for about an hour. Freeze the rest of the solution in a container and transfer to syringes when you have some more available.

Adding a Foraging Area

The test tube serves as an excellent nest for the ants. When several worker ants have emerged, they will need an additional area where they can forage.

In the wild, worker ants leave their nests to forage for food. This means that your worker ants need to leave their artificial test tube nest to forage for food.

A small container serves this purpose during this transition period. Simply place the test tube within a small container.

You can place food in the container – this will enable the workers to explore outside of the test tube and forage for food. You will also be able to remove waste that the ants will leave in this area.

At this stage, there is still no need to provide the ants with water as it is still available within the test tube.

How Much Food?

It is difficult to say exactly how much food to provide since this will depend on the size of your colony. A colony that is just starting up with just one generation of workers will only need a tiny drop of sugar water and a fruit fly each day.

Overfeeding is not problematic with ants – they will simply not take the food. There will be no harm caused, providing you clear away any uneaten food. Ensure that the foraging area is clean at all times.

In contrast, if you underfeed your ants, the growth rate of your colony will go into decline.

A substantial colony of ants can eat a surprising amount of food.

A Moldy Test Tube

If there is a buildup of mold within the test tube, you will need to transfer the ants to a new clean test tube as soon as possible.

The simplest way to facilitate this move is to join two test tubes together – attach a new test tube set up to the original one that is now displaying some mold.

It is important to allow the ants to make the move on their own – you simply need to provide the new test tube and the ants will do the rest.

The workers will find the new clean test tube and will move on their own. They will also transfer the queen and the brood by themselves!

The ants tend to be aware of any build-up of mold and will initiate the move to a clean test tube as long as it is provided. However, note that ants can tolerate a certain amount of mold – a little mold is harmless. If the mold gets to the point that you can no longer see that the cotton ball is white because of mold build up, you know you have a problem. The ants will know it too and will be keen to move.

If you are unable to attach the test tubes together, consider taping the test tubes together. Just be sure to allow some air in every now and again.

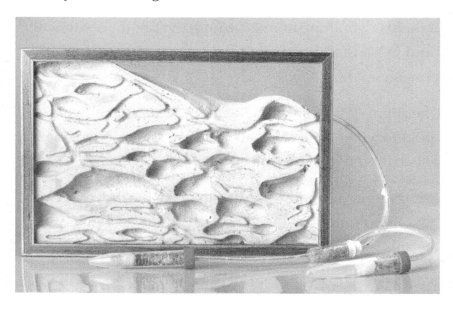

Chapter Nine - Avoid Escaping Ants

Containment

The issue of escaping ants becomes crucial both when adding a foraging area to a test tube nest – and when you have a main formicarium with an outworld. The outworld is the foraging area which will be well used by the worker ants in the colony.

Both the foraging area alongside a test tube nest and the outworld alongside a formicarium are both ordinarily open containers.

There are several advantages to keeping the foraging space as an open area. The foraging area will be used as a place to discard waste including prey carcasses and dead ants. This is an area where you need to be able to access to keep it clean.

Because there will be high humidity levels in both the nest and the foraging are, the potential for mold and unpleasant odors would increase with a lidded container. It is beneficial to allow some air to circulate.

Very importantly, you need access to this area to provide food for your ants. There will be less disturbance and subsequently stress caused to the ants if there is no need to take off and then replace a lid.

Additionally, when the colony is established in higher numbers, the foraging area will be full of ants. It would become impossible for the ant keeper to lift the lid to feed the ants without many ants escaping.

Having an open container full of crawling ants inevitably means that containment becomes a main issue in ant care. Especially as one escaped ant can lead the entire colony to move on!

Digging is very important to ants and if a foraging ant escapes and finds a good place to dig – it can lead to a mass exodus. Indeed, the scope for digging outside the formicarium is surprisingly limitless – under the house, outside the window, underneath carpets or behind baseboards.

Securing the Habitat

The habitat you provide for your ants needs to be 100% secure. Take an extremely careful look at the formicarium you intend to use – whether this is purchased from a shop or hand made.

If you notice any gaps, you will need to seal them. Consider using silicone or strong packing tape.

Chapter Nine - Avoid Escaping Ants

The following are techniques used by ant keepers to prevent ants from escaping. These methods apply to both the box containing the test tube and the main formicarium with an open outworld.

By Messor structor at the English language Wikipedia, CC BY-SA 3.0, https://commons.wikimedia.org/w/index.php?curid=2994693

Talcum Powder

Surprisingly, talcum powder or baby powder can keep ants contained within an open enclosure. This means that you can feed the ants without disturbing them and minimize the risk of ants making their escape.

However, there are some significant drawbacks in using powders.

It is very easy to accidentally brush off the powder leaving an easy escape path for your ants.

Additionally, high humidity impacts on the effectiveness of this method. Indeed, condensation can cause all of the powder to wash away completely.

Crucially, ensure that not too much powder is used. Otherwise, chunks can break off and fall in the foraging area – this is very dangerous for the ants as they can become coated in the powder and will very likely die.

If you decide to try this technique, mix the talcum powder with rubbing alcohol and smear around the edges. Create a thin paste – using a paintbrush, spread it across the upper sides of the container.

The alcohol will evaporate quickly, and the talcum powder will act as a barrier for your ants. The ants will be prevented from climbing up the talcum powder coated walls – when touched, the particles of talcum powder will fall off (along with the ant).

Ensure that the paste is not too thick. When the paste is too thick, the talcum powder particles tend to stick together so that the ant will be able to walk over the top of it. Also, there is a risk that if the paste is too thick, the ant will become coated in and will be at risk of dying.

Vaseline and Oils

Another option in how to prevent ants from making their escape is to use Vaseline (petroleum gel). This should be smeared over any tiny cracks or open areas. Cover a two-inch wide band around the outworld door plus its joints.

Whilst the vast majority of ants will not walk through it, be aware that some of the larger ant species will be able to walk over the Vaseline with ease.

Some ant keepers have had success using extra virgin olive oil. This is suitable for larger ants. However, the smaller ant species may get stuck in the oil which may result in their death.

If applying oil, coat around the edge in a one-inch band.

Chapter Nine - Avoid Escaping Ants

Some ant keepers use other methods to prevent ants from escaping such as paraffin oil. This technique seems to be particularly widespread in Europe.

Fluon

If all of these methods fail, you can use Fluon or a substance called PTFE. However, note that before these substances dry out, the fumes emitted will be fatal to ants. Ensure that you apply it in a highly ventilated area away from your ants.

Fluon can be purchased online through a website called Bioquip – fluon is referred to as 'Insect-a-Slip Insect Barrier. It is widely used in laboratories working with insects.

Moats

Moats filled with water can also function as a barrier to escaping ants.

The vast majority of ants will avoid water at all costs – they may even try to put things on top of the water in attempt to prevent the water from advancing towards them.

However, some ants can swim. Find out more about the species you are keeping before considering using a moat.

Another concern is the risk of ants accidentally drowning in the moat. Indeed, ants are capable of drowning in a droplet of water placed in a feeding dish – there is always the risk of exploring ants drowning and dying in the moat.

Using a Lid

Another option is simply to use a lid that seals the outworld.

Ensure that there are holes in the lid to allow for adequate ventilation.

Also, remember that your ants will experience stress with any disturbance caused by taking the lid off and then replacing it. Consider how much change in light there will be for your ants, and the amount of vibration / movement there will be.

Ants will be happy and thrive in an environment where there is as little disturbance as possible.

This explains why so many ant keepers prefer to avoid the use of lids. There is also the issue of escaping ants when you do remove the lid for feeding and cleaning purposes. This time will provide a possible escape route for your ants.

Ant Farms - The Ultimate Formicarium Handbook --Page 92

Encourage your Ants to Stay Put

In addition to the above methods, ensure that you are meeting all of your ant's needs. Although not scientifically proven, it does appear that ants are far less likely to try and escape if they have everything they need within their habitat.

Ensure that you go to great lengths to minimize disturbance such as light and vibrations when feeding.

Also, try experimenting with different diets. If you notice that your foraging ants are trying to climb out, it could be that they are trying to find something that they cannot locate within their habitat.

For example, they may be in search of a source of sugar or protein that is not available to them.

When an ant has found what they need (for example a food source), they will leave a trail of pheromones to show other workers to the food source. The aim is that if the ants have what they need, there will be no need to keep searching.

Ants that appear to be trying to escape could also be looking for somewhere dark (and restful).

Alternatively, a worker ant that is sick will often try and leave the colony to die.

Chapter Ten – Managing your Formicarium

The Ant Farm

A formicarium that is designed to house a queen ant and her colony will be comprised of two separate sections. With your support, the ants will be able to sustain themselves for many years. The queen can produce millions of eggs in her lifetime.

The formicarium will contain a nest area which is where the queen and her brood reside – and an outdoor area where the worker ants will come to forage.

The foraging area, often referred to as the outworld or basin is a place where the worker ants can leave their nests and come to explore and forage. This is a perfect set-up – you can add the food to the outworld and clear any waste away – without opening and disturbing the nest area with the queen and the brood.

Chapter Ten – Managing your Formicarium

The outworld for your colony should be as large as possible and kept open. It should offer more space than the nest. This is because this area is imitating the foraging ground – the world outside of the nest.

A spacious outworld tends to encourage more natural and interesting behaviors – including ants creating very elaborate trails to and from food.

You can distribute food for you ants in this outworld – live or freshly killed insects, fruit, honey mixed with water soaked into a cotton ball, and meats.

Ensure that you remove any uneaten food to maintain cleanliness and hygiene within the outworld. Additionally, the ants will utilize particular areas for storing dead ants – discard these as soon as possible to prevent rotting.

Caring for a colony in a formicarium becomes quite different to caring for a single queen or even an evolving colony.

Now the colony is beginning to establish itself and the different ants take up their separate roles within the colony. This is the time when the ants need a variety of foods, plenty of space, an outworld – also possibly a moisture gradient and a temperature gradient (see chapter eleven).

There are many different and decent designs of formicarium's available – these you can purchase in stores or online. Ant colony starter kits are available which include both the test tube start-ups as well as the larger formicarium.

Excellent online stores include Ants Canada, Ant Store and Tar Heel Ants – among many others.

When you are looking at buying your ant farm, find out if there is a way to provide humidity to the nest. This is usually a sponge which you need to keep moist (dampen with water every few days) or a water tower. This will help to keep the nest humid which will increase the colony survival rate.

Many ant keepers choose to make and design their own formicarium and there are many online tutorials available which will show you how.

There are also many different designs that you can look at online to get an idea of how you would like yours to look. Websites to look at include The Ant Farm Forum – www.tapatalk.com/groups/antfarm ; Ant Store – www.antstore.net/forum ; and Ants Canada – www.antscanada.com

In a formicarium, the nest area is normally made of gypsum or concrete and has tunnels in it. This would be covered by a glass slate. The glass would usually be covered by something to keep the nest dark – but can be uncovered so that the ant keeper can look inside the nest.

The outside compartment is where the worker ants come to forage. Here you would leave food for the ants – and the ants would leave you waste that you would need to clear away.

Both the nest area and the outside section are protected against ants escaping by shutting it off or covering the outside edges with a protective coating of your choice (see previous chapter, Avoid Escaping Ants).

Before embarking on such a venture, it is essential to understand the ant's nest in the natural environment.

Understanding the Ant Nest

The purpose of the ant's nest is to protect and shelter the ants from predators as well as from the weather. They provide a safe place for the ants to rear their brood and to keep the queen protected. Ants would not be able to survive for long without their nest.

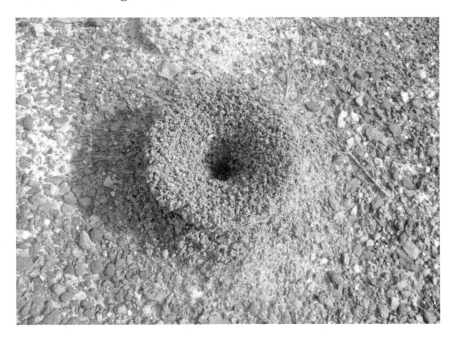

The majority of ant nests are dug into damp soil. They can be several feet deep and also in circumference. Nests can also be made out of wood pulp which is chewed into a paper like substance. This is similar to the way that wasps make their nests.

Some ant nests are build inside the stem of plants. Nests can even be made out of a ball of leaves – where leaves are joined together by the worker ants. The ants use their larvae as silk thread producers.

Some ant nests are inconspicuous with only one entrance in the ground that is quite well hidden. Other ant nests are very noticeable. For example, the southern Wood Ant, *Formica rufa,* make large mounds of earth and pine needles. These can be several feet high, and contain many entrances and exits.

Ants Building Nests

The complexity and intricacy of the ant nest tends to vary amongst different species of ants. Some species tend to dig only a few tunnels and chambers. In contrast, other species build very elaborate nests with many chambers of different sizes and countless interconnecting tunnels.

Ants dig and build their nests by biting a little piece soil using their jaws. They then carry the soil outside of the nest. Sometimes they also use their front feet to carry it out. Individual ants remove the soil that they bite themselves (as opposed to passing it onto another worker ant). This means that there is some inevitable jostling as the tunnels are built – this is very normal behavior.

Chapter Ten – Managing your Formicarium

The time taken to build the nest depends on how many worker ants there are in the colony – also how large and intricate the nest is that is being built. It can take anywhere from just a few days to several weeks to complete their nest.

Additionally, if a colony is able to grow (where a queen is present), the ants will remain busy working on the nest's expansion. This is especially prevalent when the large flying ants start to emerge.

Controlling the Nest's Environment

The ants control their own environment within the nest. For example, they open and close various entrances to the nest to control how much air circulates in the nest.

The lower parts of the nest tend to be cooler and often damper. The worker ants will move the brood from various parts of the nest when it becomes too cool, warm, wet, or dry for the larvae.

This illustrates how important it is that you do not dig into the ant nest when you are searching for a queen ant. There is a huge risk that you will have a detrimental impact on the entire colony.

During cold periods, some ant species hibernate. During hibernation, the ants close all entrances to the nest. They move down to the bottom of the nest where it is warmer and further away from frozen soil, winter frosts and snow.

The majority of ant species will fight to defend their nests against predators and any dangers. However, there are certain species that tend to evacuate the nest, taking their brood and queen away from the threat.

Sometimes, ants can invade another ant nest – attacking and killing the ants that built the nest and then taking it over.

Moving from the Test Tube to the New Formicarium

This can be an immediate process or a gradual one depending on the ants!

Some ant nests available (such as through Ants Canada) have a facility where you can attach the test tube containing your ant colony directly into your new formicarium.

Another option is to place the test tube directly into the outlying area (foraging space) which is connected to the new formicarium. Move the opening of the test tube close to the opening of the tube that leads to the nest.

Where the ants appear reluctant to make the move, you could shine a light onto the test tube. Cover the new nest area so that is lovely and dark – and consequently much more welcoming to the ants.

The process of moving the ants to their new formicarium can seem a little slow but they will eventually make the transition. Once they do, you will find that they leave the test tube completely empty of ants and brood. You can then remove the test tube.

Acorn Ant island / Fractality/ Flickr - https://www.flickr.com/photos/fractality23/8838921501

Building up the Colony

It is impossible to predict how long it will take for a single queen to build up to a large ant colony. This depends on the species of ant and is also affected by temperature and diet.

Ant colonies that are kept a few degrees above room temperature – and are also well fed, tend to develop faster. The queen generally lays more eggs (and more frequently) and the brood develop into adult ants at an increased rate.

The first worker ants are known as 'nanitics'. They normally emerge a few weeks after the queen is established in her nest. It can take between several months and a year for the colony to have a plentiful amount of worker ants.

Feeding the Colony

Just like feeding the nanitic worker ants and the ants of an emerging colony, ants within a larger and growing colony continue to enjoy dead or live insects and a mix of sugar water (or honey and water).

Suitable insects to offer include freshly dead or live fruit flies, small crickets, flies, moths and aphids. The proteins in these insects are critical for maintaining the strength and well-being of your colony.

It is also beneficial to offer a variety of insects. By offering a choice and a wide range, you will soon be able to see what your ants are keen to feed on – and if there is anything they are not so keen on. Additionally, a range of different insects will guarantee that your ants are consuming enough protein.

Note that it is not recommended to feed your ants wild insects that you catch from outside. This is due to the risk that these insects have encountered pesticides or are carrying diseases. To avoid your pet ants consuming pesticides and spreading potential diseases, offer insects that you have purchased from a pet store or online. Many ant keepers also raise insects such as fruit flies or cockroaches that they can feed to their ants.

Alternative protein sources for ants include cooked chicken, cat or dog food, boiled or scrambled eggs.

Some species (such as the harvester ant *Messor barbarous*), like to eat seeds. This can be offered alongside the insects and sugar water. Occasionally, you could offer a piece of fruit, a piece of meat, pollen or syrup.

Pour your sugar water into the lid of a soda bottle and place this in the outside area of your formicarium. Ensure that you replace this water every 2 to 3 days; and check that it does not run out.

Chapter Eleven - Humidity and Temperature

Optimum Humidity

The ideal level of humidity for an ant colony depends on the species. Some ant species thrive in a nest that is dry while other species flourish in a nest that is moist.

The ants intuitively recognize the level of humidity that they require. This means that you can guarantee the optimum level by offering them different moisture levels within the nest.

You will even see that the ants will move the brood to an area of the nest that has optimum humidity.

The main difficulty with getting the humidity level correct is knowing what the optimum level is for the species of ants you are keeping.

Most stores will provide you with specific information on the species that they sell.

Due to restrictions on the sale of queen ants in the USA, you are most likely keeping a species which is native to your local area. Aim to provide a similar habitat to your local environment. If purchasing, you will be buying through a GAN farmer who will be able to advise you. If you find the ants yourself, try and replicate the environment where you found the ants.

Additionally, you may be able to find information on ants of the same genus or ants from similar habitats – this would give you a reasonable indication.

Ultimately, by observing your ants, you will soon be able to work out the correct humidity level.

For example, if the nest appears dry (the plaster is light and seems powdery), you need to increase the humidity levels.

Alternatively, if large amounts of water begin to accumulate on the glass due to condensation, you need to lower the humidity level.

Adjusting Humidity Levels

Within the nest, humidity levels are dependent on moisture content. Ideally, one part of the formicarium should be moist and another part much dryer. This allows the ants the opportunity to move to different parts of the nest dependent on their need for different humidity levels.

Humidity levels are especially critical for a large colony. This is because the different ants, eggs, pupae and larvae all have varying optimal humidity levels.

Chapter Eleven - Humidity and Temperature

Within the nest, the degree of humidity is determined by the moisture level. It can be added by allowing water to evaporate.

In the simple test-tube nest, the dampened cotton wool provided the queen and emerging colony with moisture.

Many shop bought formicarium's have an inbuilt way of adjusting the humidity levels such as a water tower or an area with a sponge that you will need to keep moist.

In a larger formicarium, you are also providing moisture through regular feeding and water feeders. Surprisingly, a simple droplet of water (0.5 ml) squirted into the formicarium will increase humidity levels. Some ant keepers will use a water spray to gently create mist in one area of the formicarium.

Moist cotton wool balls, sponge, water chamber, wick, water towers, water feeders and spraying with water will all help to contribute to raising the humidity levels. Ideally, cotton wool balls should be placed inside a test tube and kept within the outworld / foraging area.

Humidity is also affected by the amount of aeration in the formicarium – one that is lidded is more likely to retain moisture and therefore have a higher humidity level.

Keeping the correct temperate also impacts on the level of humidity. If you find that the moisture level is too low, try keeping the formicarium a little warmer. Conversely, if the moisture level is too high try keeping the formicarium a little cooler.

You can purchase digital hygrometers (usually combined with a digital thermometer) so you can keep a check on the humidity percentage. This is especially useful if you can find out the desired humidity level for the species you are keeping.

How Feeding is Connected to Humidity Levels

Although humidity levels need to be higher in the nest, humidity levels are still critical in the foraging area.

Some ants will only be able to feed on soft food – this is particularly prevalent in younger colonies where the worker ants lack the strength to consume food that may have dried out. It is generally preferable to offer mostly liquid food sources until the colony becomes established with a multitude of workers. Liquid food sources include sugar water as well as cutting open crickets, flies and mealworms.

The Problem with Too Much Humidity

Too much humidity inevitably means a buildup of mold.

This is a serious problem for ants and will result in their death.

Ensure that you remove uneaten food. Also pay careful attention to damp cotton wool balls that will eventually go moldy and will need replacing.

One indication that your humidity level is too high is if water droplets form on the formicarium glass.

The temperature of the room you keep your formicarium in will have a significant impact on humidity levels. If you notice that humidity levels are too high, as well as reducing water evaporation / moisture content in the formicarium, consider whether you can move the ants to a cooler room in your home.

The Problem with Too Little Humidity

Too little humidity in the nest causes a different set of problems.

Firstly, too little humidity can mean that foods dry out very quickly. This makes it difficult for the ants to feed from them. They are more likely to drag the food into the nest to feed the colony where humidity levels are higher. Once the food has been taken inside the nest, you will not be able to remove / clean it away. This unavoidably results in serious problems with mold and decay.

Too little humidity also makes the ants need to work harder to stay hydrated. The ants would also experience difficulties in raising the brood. This will impact on brood development. During periods of dryness, ants are even known to eat the brood.

Optimum Temperature

The ideal temperature for a formicarium tends to be between 20 and 28 degrees. The ants will tolerate a drop in nighttime temperature to about 15 degrees without any detrimental impact.

The ideal temperature varies of course on the type of ant species you are keeping. Since you will be keeping ants from your local area, use the natural outside temperatures as your guide – try and keep the ants at a similar temperature to the outside world.

Many ant keepers choose to heat the nest with an electric heat mat or with a lamp. Whilst the nest area needs to remain dark, it is okay to direct a heat lamp towards the nest as long as it is covered with material to keep it dark (such as black plastic or paper).

Be aware that this can be a fire hazard though – and it is extremely important not to overheat the ant nest as this will result in fatalities amongst your ants.

Chapter Twelve – Different Ant Species

Which Species to Choose

There are more than 12,000 different species of ants all over the world. Even in a single region, there can be thousands of different species.

Fortunately, there is no one species that is 'the best' for keeping at home. Indeed, almost all species can be kept successfully by ant keepers – providing they have the right housing, food and care.

It is a good idea to find out which ants are a common species in your area. This is especially relevant if you are planning to locate and source them yourself. This way you will have an idea about the species of ants you are likely to be cultivating.

It is not possible or advisable to mix different species of ants in one formicarium. They will undoubtedly fight, and many ants will die as a consequence. Even ants that are of the same species but from a different colony will fight – they regard each other as a threat.

Colonies identify each other through scent – ants within the same colony have a specific scent. Any ant that does not share the same scent will be treated as an adversary and they will definitely fight.

Due to the enormous possibilities of species available to you, we have only included a short description of a few species. You will be able to see how the care and maintenance varies between species.

Here are some of the easiest and more popular ant species to keep – they are perfect for beginners as well as experts.

Lasius Niger

The *Lasius Niger* are frequently named Black Garden Ants.

They are widespread across North America, Europe and some parts of Easter Asia.

Typically, they are easy to find as they make their nests in dirt or under stones. They can be found in many backyards, parks and underneath pavement slabs.

They are the perfect species for an ant keeper who is just starting out – they are low maintenance, extremely tough, active, long lasting, clean, easy to find and unable to bite or sting.

Temperament:

Typically, these ants are very active and fastmoving.

Very gentle towards humans. They do not bite or sting.
They tend to run away and try to avoid human
confrontation.

In the natural environment, they tend to find their strength
in numbers – they have large colonies with lots of workers.

Like many ant species, they can be very vicious towards
other insects.

Diet:

Lasius Niger are easy ants to feed as they tend to eat anything! Include soft fruits, seeds and other small insects in their diet.

Many farmers and allotment owners see the *Lasius Niger* as a pest as they enjoy feeding on soft fruits such as strawberries. They also farm aphids and scale, nurturing and protecting them in return for the honeydew they excrete. The ants carry the aphids and scale from host plant to host plant; effectively spreading these garden pests to new healthy plants.

During the early summer months, black garden ant workers tend to be very thorough in their search for food. This is to try and increase the food supply for the queen and her brood. The ants will readily burrow through bricks and mortar, searching homes for food supplies. They have been blamed for causing weaknesses in building foundations.

Colony:

The queen has a notably fast rate of reproduction – meaning that there will be a lot of workers in your formicarium.

A thriving colony can have as many as 10,000 worker ants after a few years.

Queen:

The queen is around 9mm, with dark brown/black legs and antenna with a hint of red.

Like many other ant species, *Lasius Niger* is monogamous. This means that a single colony will host only one queen. If another queen is introduced to the nest, it will result in conflict and death.

The entire colony is dependent on the one queen.

The queen is fully claustral – she will not need any additional food or nutrients before the first generation of workers emerge. All that she will need is water.

Workers:

The workers are between 3 to 5mm. They are black with reddish legs and antenna.

Hibernation:

This species resides in temperate zones which means that they hibernate during the winter.

Hibernation would ordinarily last from October to March. During this time, the formicarium should ideally be kept between 5 and 10 degrees Celsius.

Lifespan:

The Lasius Niger queens have a very long expected lifespan of about 15 years, but they can even live for an amazing 30 years.

Camponotus

The *Camponotus* are known as Carpenter Ants. They are another extremely popular species amongst ant farmers and are ideal for beginners.

They are one of the largest of all ant species. The colony is polymorphic which makes the colony very diverse and fascinating to observe (see following section on 'workers').

Chapter Twelve – Different Ant Species

Carpenter ants are indigenous to many forested parts of the world and there are over 1,000 different species. They are found across the United States.

Colonies are usually found within moist logs and tree stumps, basically any dead and damp wood. They commonly make nests in wooden buildings and structures, and are regarded as a major cause of structural damage.

One of the most common species in the United States is the black carpenter ant – *Camponotus pennsylvanicus.*

By Muhammad Mahdi Karim - Own work by Author, GFDL 1.2, https://commons.wikimedia.org/w/index.php?curid=6139103

Temperament:

Carpenter ants are completely harmless to humans, they do not bite or sting.

Diet:

These ants are easy to feed, and they enjoy a varied diet. They will eat insects, fruits and sugar or honey water. In their natural environment, carpenter ants consume a lot of honeydew (produced by aphids).

One of the most common misunderstandings about the Carpenter ant is that they consume wood. Although they chew wood to make their homes, they do not eat the wood but rather spit it out.

Colony:

The *Camponotus* take a long time to become an established colony. Indeed, it usually takes over a year before you can move them from the test tube nest to your formicarium.

It is believed that these ants take longer to develop as they are much larger than most other species. For example, it takes two months for this type of ant to develop from egg to worker – in most species, this process takes only one month.

Chapter Twelve – Different Ant Species

A Carpenter ant colony will need between 20 to 50 workers before it can be moved from test tube to formicarium. There will usually be growth in the second year after they have been moved into the formicarium – and then more rigorous growth in the third year. It takes about 3 – 4 years for the colony to be considered as fully mature.

Colonies tend to be comprised of between 3,000 and 6,000 worker ants.

Queen:

The queen can grow to 20 mm in length.

Queens are completely claustral. Indeed, you will not need to feed the queen until after she has laid her first batch of eggs.

Another reason for slow colony growth is because the queen lays eggs in batches, taking breaks in between each batch of eggs. The breaks can be several weeks – or even months. This is unusual in comparison to other ant species.

Queens are monogamous so there can only be one queen within the colony.

Workers:

Adult worker ants can measure between 6 and 12 mm in length.

The Carpenter ants are polymorphic. This means that different workers are assigned to specific tasks – this is then reflected in varying sizes of the worker ants. Indeed, the workers come in many different shapes and sizes.

The minor workers are responsible for nest duties which include taking care of the queen and the brood.

The major workers and super majors cut up large pieces of food and return it for the colony to share. In their natural world, the major workers would also serve as soldiers to defend against predators.

Hibernation:

The *Camponotus* hibernate during the winter. This further contributes to slow colony growth. Indeed, hibernation initiates another pause in egg laying – an additional period of inactivity.

Lifespan

Like all ant species, lifespan of the carpenter ants depends on their position in the nest.

Queens can live for over 10 years.

The lifespan of the female workers varies massively - between just a few months and a staggering 7 years.

Tetramorium

Tetramorium are often referred to as Pavement Ants. Their name stems from the fact they frequently make their homes in pavement. Native to Europe, these ants now reside in urban areas across North America and Europe.

Although they were introduced to North America as a pest, they are not a threat to native insect species and have not had any kind of detrimental impact on their adopted environments.

1 mm

By The photographer and www.AntWeb.org, CC BY 4.0,
https://commons.wikimedia.org/w/index.php?curid=8114596

The *Tetramorium* ants are low maintenance and are tolerant to a wide range of conditions.

For pavement ants to thrive, a hydration gradient within the formicarium will be essential. This is because these ants like to choose their own moisture levels.

To achieve a hydration gradient, you will need to keep one side of the nest wet and keep the other side dry. This allows the ants to reside in their desired level of humidity. See Chapter 11 – 'Humidity and Temperature' for further information.

Reproduction can also be increased by providing a temperature gradient within the nest. This can be attained by installing a heating cable or heat mat to one side of the nest.

Temperament:

Tetramorium are particularly fastmoving and active ants.

They are much smaller than the *Camponotus*. The fact that they are small and fastmoving means that cleaning their enclosure can be more of a challenge.

The *Tetramorium* have tiny stingers on their abdomen. The stingers are used to subdue prey. However, their stingers are not large enough to penetrate through human skin. This makes them easy for ant keepers to handle.

Diet:

Pavement ants feed on a hugely diverse range of foods including sugary foodstuffs (such as nectar, fruit and sugar or honey water), other insects and grains, seeds and nuts.

In their natural habitats, pavement ants tend to consume just about anything they can find – insects, seeds, honeydew, honey, bread, meat, nuts, ice cream and cheese. They also hunt for and consume codling moth larvae.

Colony:

A *Tetramorium* colony will expand incredibly quickly. A nest can consist of around 10,000 workers.

In the outdoor world, the pavement ants tend to exhibit very aggressive behavior towards other colonies.

During early spring, colonies endeavor to take over new areas and will frequently attack nearby colonies to do so. Inevitably, this aggressive behavior leads to enormous battles – sometimes resulting in the death of thousands of ants.

During the heat of summer, the *Tetramorium* ants dig out the sand in between the pavements. This is to provide ventilation for the nest.

Queen:

The Pavement ant queen is approximately 8 mm long, at least twice the size of the worker ants.

She is fully claustral which means she will not need feeding until the worker ants have emerged.

The queen will lay eggs continuously throughout her life, producing many brood. She will also lay eggs very quickly after hibernation. This differs to other species where there is usually a slight delay in egg laying following hibernation.

The *Tetramorium* queens are mostly monogamous (with only one queen per nest) but occasionally a nest may consist of two or more queens.

Workers:

Pavement ants have dark brown / blackish bodies with pale legs. On average, worker ants are around 3.25 mm.

All the worker ants are of equal size as the colony is monomorphic.

The role of the young ants is to tend to the queen and the brood. As the eggs hatch and the ants emerge, they will spend the following two to three months in the nest.

The queen does not look after her brood in any sense – her only function is to lay the eggs. The young female workers tend to and care for both the queen and the brood – eggs, larvae and pupae.

At around four months old, the worker ants take on a new role within the colony – foraging and hunting for food; and defending the colony. This is when they begin to leave the nest.

Hibernation:

The *Tetramorium* species tend to hibernate during the winter months of November through to February.

Lifespan:

Pavement worker ants tend to live for approximately five years. The queen will live for a much longer time.

Myrmica Rubra

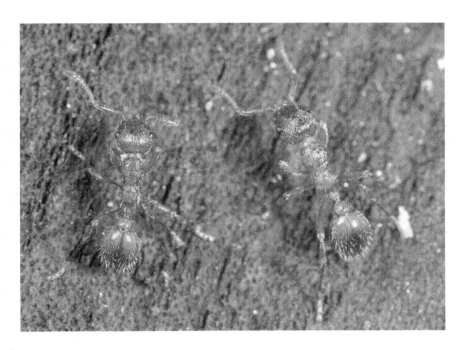

By Gary Alpert at English Wikipedia, CC BY 2.5,
https://commons.wikimedia.org/w/index.php?curid=3387868

The *Myrmica rubra* are commonly known as red ants – the European fire ant, or the common red ant. This species is found in parts of North America, across Europe and in Asia.

Red ants tend to reside in coastal regions; or areas where there is a lot of water, such as the Great Lakes or near rivers. They flourish in damp environments. Red ants are inclined to make their nests under stones, within fallen trees and in soil or soft dirt. They are incredibly adaptable and can make their nests out of virtually any material.

These ants are ideal for ant keepers as they are low maintenance and easy to find. They are extremely tough and highly active.

Temperament:

The *Myrmica rubra* tend to be very aggressive. Instead of running away, these ants will usually attack to defend themselves – by stinging.

The sting is similar to that of a nettle sting – besides some discomfort, the stings are actually harmless to humans (unless you experience an allergic reaction). Stinging can be described as a slight burning sensation – it can last between just a few hours or an entire day.

However, note that there are some red ant species that do not sting.

Diet:

Red stinging ants are fierce predators and eat other small insects. They also farm honeydew from aphids. This is like the *Lasius Niger* (black garden ants).

Offer a diet including live and dead insects (flies, mealworms, crickets, cockroaches and many more) and honey or sugar water. For protein, you can also offer meat such as cooked chicken. The *Myrmica rubra* tend to thrive on a diet rich in protein.

Freshwater should always be provided.

Colony:

Colonies are large and usually highly active. In their natural habitat, established red ant colonies have been found with an incredible 250,000 worker ants and multiple queens. In the wild, there can be up to 100 queens per colony.

In a well-established formicarium, you can expect up to 20,000 worker ants.

Growth and expansion in the colony tends to be quite rapid as there are multiple queens.

The *Myrmica rubra* prefer highly moistened nests.

Queen:

The *Myrmica rubra* queen is dark red and measures approximately 5 to 7 mm. Because the queens are only marginally larger than the worker ants, the queens can be difficult to identify.

The red ants are c which means there are multiple queens within the colony.

Each individual queen tends to lay fewer eggs than the other ant species we have covered - but this is compensated by the fact that you can keep more than one queen.

Occasionally, these queens will lay a very substantial batch of eggs and will then undergo a period of inactivity. Some of the queens are quite slow in laying their first batch of eggs. Once your queen has started laying eggs, it will take about 6 weeks for the first workers to arrive.

Note that although these ants are polygynous, it is very risky to add an additional queen to the colony. Ordinarily, the new queen will be rejected and attacked, resulting in her death.

The *Myrmica rubra* queen in semi-claustral. This means that she will need some nourishment during the initial breeding stages. Sugar or honey water is generally sufficient.

Be careful not to offer an excess of food as this will go moldy. Remove any uneaten food but remember that your ant will also benefit from as little disturbance as possible – just a minute drop of sugar or honey water is ample. If the queen experiences any level of stress due to disturbance, it is very likely that she will delay egg laying – and there is a risk that she will even begin eating her own eggs.

Workers:

The red ant workers measure between 4 and 5 mm. The workers are of the same size, no majors and minors.

These worker ants are dark red.

Hibernation:

These ants will need to hibernate between the end of October until March. During hibernation, the ants should be kept at a temperature between 5 and 8 degrees Celcius.

Lifespan:

The *Myrmica rubra* queen can live for as long as 15 years.

Formica fusca

The Formica fusca are sometimes referred to as Slave ants or Helper ants. They can be found in Northern areas of the United States, also residing throughout Canada and across Europe.

Like the Carpenter ants, the *Formica* live in wooded habitats. They are inclined to make their colonies on the forest ground, or underneath rocks and logs. They will also nest in open fields.

The *Formica* are comparatively large. They are an easy species to keep with low daily maintenance and with high resilience. With lots of protein sources on offer, they are sure to thrive.

This species would benefit from a small heater mat with an ideal temperature being between 18 and 28 degrees Celsius for the arena and between 24 to 28 degrees Celsius for the nest.

The term 'Slave ants' derives from their unique behavior. Some of the worker ants will seek out other colonies to attack – if successful, all the ants from that colony will become their 'slaves'.

Temperament:

These ants are very active and fast moving.

Like other *Formica* species, *Formica fusca* can spray formic acid from the end of their gasters. They do not use formic acid very frequently – but when they feel under threat or attack, they are able to release this acid. If the colony is put under a lot of stress, the workers may emit formic acid. Ensure that you do not get any formic acid into your eyes as it can really sting.

These ants are also able to bite – disagreeable but harmless to humans.

Diet:

The *Formica fusca* will consume many different insects (such as mealworms, bluebottle flies, fruit flies, spiders, wasps, bees, moths, crickets, waxworms, locusts, beetles and even other ant species). Meat such as cooked chicken and also boiled eggs, serve as excellent source of protein.

Additionally, they will benefit from sugary foodstuffs such as apple slices and sugar or honey water.

Protein is particularly important for a developing brood and the colony will need plenty to be able to thrive.

In their natural habitat, *Formica fusca* feed on small insects such as codling moth larvae, aphid honeydew and extrafloral nectaries.

Colony:

An established colony is smaller than most, consisting of between 500 and 2000 worker ants.

Disturbance to the nest should be kept to an absolute minimum – if the colony is put under a lot of stress, the workers will spread formic acid which can result in death.

Queen:

The *Formica fusca* queen measures about 12 mm. She is shiny gray / black in color with brown / red legs.

The queen is fully-claustral which means that she will not need any additional food or nourishment until the first worker ants arrive.

The *Fomica fusca* colonies can either be monogamous or polygynous. However, it is often the case that the colony begins with two queens raising their first brood or workers together, but then when the workers emerge, the queens attack each other until one dies.

Sometimes the queen will not lay eggs until after hibernation – this is especially true where the queen mated in a late nuptial flight (late summer / early fall).

Workers:

The worker ants measure between 4 and 8 mm. Like the queen, they are shiny gray / black in color.

There is no division in the worker ants with majors and minors.

Hibernation:

These ants should hibernate throughout the winter and will wake from hibernation around late March.

During hibernation, the ants should be kept at around 8 degrees Celsius, but no colder than this.

Lifespan:

The lifespan of the queen is generally between 10 and 15 years.

Identifying Ants

Both beginners to ant keeping and experienced myrmecologists find it difficult to identify different species of ants. This is largely because there is such a vast range of species.

A useful website to refer to is Taxonomers.com – it enables other fellow ant keepers to help you identify your ants.

The site also collects data about nuptial flights. The site follows environmental factors such as weather, elevation, location, time of day, time of year to make predictions about when nuptial flights will occur.

The AntsCanada forum website is also hugely helpful in identifying ants.

Chapter Thirteen – A Growing Colony

Suitable Nest Size

Although it is tempting to think that by providing a large nest, you will encourage your colony to expand, it is not actually true.

A small ant colony will only need a small ant nest. If the nest is too big, the ants will store their garbage (waste food and dead ants) in the hallways and chambers. This will be impossible for you to clean and will result in a build-up of mold. This will eventually be fatal to your ants.

The ideal scenario is for the ants to grow into their nests – simply wait for the colony to expand and then move them into a bigger nest.

If there is enough food and the conditions are correct, the ant colony will keep expanding regardless of the size of the nest.

When your colony is fully established, and you no longer wish it to expand, you can restrict the growth of the colony by limiting the amount of food you give. Additionally, lower the temperate slightly. Combined, this will keep the colony at the size you desire.

Winged Ants

Surprisingly, ants that are kept in a formicarium do not leave the nest on mass for their nuptial flight, like they do in the natural environment.

Consequently, your ants will not depart your colony for an annual nuptial flight.

It is considered that this is because there are specific environmental changes that trigger the ants to prepare for nuptial flights. It is thought that triggers include temperature changes, humidity levels, photoperiod (length of daylight hours).

Chapter Thirteen – A Growing Colony

In comparison to ants in the wild, ants within a formicarium are not subjected to the same changes in their environment – the conditions are kept largely constant.

As an ant keeper, you will notice that the queen will produce winged queens and males from time to time. These winged ants will leave and return to the nest, often exploring the outworld. The males tend to die after a short period, and the queens tend to break off their wings after a time – and then take on the role of a worker ant. These queens will have a similar lifespan to the other worker ants.

Occasionally males will successfully fly out of the outworld. If you are keeping ants that are not native to your local area, you will need to keep your outworld closed so that the alates will naturally die out.

However, if you are keeping ants that are native to your local area, consider moving the formicarium and outworld outside. This will give the alates an opportunity to undergo a nuptial flight and possibly begin a new colony in the wild.

Ensure that you position the formicarium and outworld in a sheltered area. Check that there is easy access for the alates to fly out of the outworld. Also, crucially, make sure that the ants cannot be rained on – and therefore be at risk of drowning.

Double the Queens?

There are some species that flourish with several queens in the nest. These are known as polygynous. However, it is more complex within a formicarium.

It is often the case that two queens will raise their young together peacefully – until the first worker ants appear.

At this point, the queens attack each other until there is only one survivor. Sometimes the worker ants will also participate in attacking the queen. The risk is that the surviving queen can suffer serious injury and it may result in neither queen surviving. This could leave your colony without a queen.

At other times, two queens living in a very large set up will habitat very different areas of the nest, establishing their own separate colonies.

Encouraging the Colony to Expand

The rate at which a colony expands is dependent on the queen's rate of egg production.

As an ant keeper, your only way to increase the queen's rate of egg production is through heat and availability of food.

Chapter Thirteen – A Growing Colony

Like all insects, ants are cold blooded. Consequently, the rate of all their physiological functions depends on the heat in their environment.

Heat Pads

Place a heat pad under one side of the nest. By heating only one side, your ants have the option to move to a cooler side depending on their needs. It is important for the ants to not be overheated.

By warming up one side of the nest to around 25 to 27 degrees C, the queen's egg production will accelerate.

Warm Location

Perhaps a simpler way to keep your ants warm is to keep the formicarium and outworld in a warm room in your house.

However, be careful to avoid direct sunlight as this will be detrimental to your ants.

Nourishment

While your colony is growing, ensure that you provide ample nourishment to guarantee maximum growth. Indeed, you can feed your ants as much as they eat. They will especially respond well to proteins (a range of insects).

However, do not feed your ants more than what they can eat. Carefully watch to ensure that the food you give is being eaten. When ants are fed in excess, they will begin storing food within their nest. This food will be left and buried – it will inevitably turn to mold and consequently be damaging to the colony.

Chapter Thirteen – A Growing Colony

Providing Water

Water is very important to ants and must always be available. However, ants will consume most of the water they require through foods such as apples, sugar or honey water and juicy insects (like mealworms and crickets). Although fruit flies are an excellent source of protein, they do not have a lot of water content.

Provide ants with water through a liquid feeder or a few drops on a dish. Note that just a few drops on a dish will boost the humidity level in the foraging area – be aware that if the humidity levels become too high, you may experience a build-up of mold.

Also, be aware that ants can drown in very little water. Ensure that a dish of water contains just a water droplet.

An alternative is to provide a test tube filled with water. Seal the end with a cotton wool ball and place the test tube in the outworld. The ants will be able to drink the water from the cotton.

Providing water to the colony serves to increase the moisture level within the colony and provides a source of drinking water for the ants. Both are crucial to the ants' wellbeing. Indeed, most ant species thrive in a moderate to very moist nest environment.

Expected Lifespan

The expected lifespan for ants depends on their caste within the colony. For example, once a drone has fulfilled its' role (fertilized a queen), it will die within a matter of days.

For the majority of ant species, the worker ants have a short lifespan consisting of a few months. However, this does vary between species – most fire ant workers live for about 6 months whereas carpenter ant workers can life for about 7 years.

Ordinarily, the larger worker ants within the colony have a longer lifespan than the smaller worker ants within the same colony. Consequently, most majors will live longer than minors. Researchers speculate that this is because the larger ants take longer to raise from egg to adult. These ants have adapted longer lifespans because the colony has invested more resources into them.

The queen ants are the fundamental lifelines of all ant colonies. Without the queen, the colony can only survive for a few months. The queen breeds the millions of ants that function together to manage and maintain the nest. Workers exist to look after the queen and the nest. They will watch over the queen and ensure that all her needs are met.

This inevitably means that the life cycle of an ant nest is dependent of the lifespan of the queen.

Queen ants have one of the longest life-spans of any known insect – sometimes as long as 30 years. This varies amongst species.

Chapter Fourteen – Ants during the Winter

Ants that Hibernate

Some ant species hibernate during the winter. Indeed, from spring to fall, ants can be seen coming and going from their nests. During the winter, entrances to the nest are closed and ants stay within the nest. This explains why you may have noticed an absence of ants in the winter time!

Because ants are cold blooded, their body temperature changes in accordance to the outdoor temperature.

During the winter time, the ant's body temperature drops meaning that all movement is inevitably very slow. They hibernate in comparatively warm places such as the soil or under the bark of trees.

During the autumn, the ants start to prepare for winter. They eat large amounts of food so that they can survive winter without food.

When the springtime brings warmth and sunshine, the ants become active and open the entrances to their nest. Now you will see them venturing outside again.

Allowing your Ants to Hibernate

To imitate the natural world, ant species that would ordinarily hibernate in the natural world, should experience hibernation of a kind in your home. This includes all species from a temperate region (which experience cold winters).

Consider that the average hibernation period is approximately 3 to 4 months. At the onset of cold weather, move the formicarium and outworld (or test tube set-up) into a cool room in the house – garage, attic, basement room (or even a fridge set at the warmest temperature).

This way, your ants can hibernate, just like they would in the wild.

Very importantly, do not simply place your ants outside during the winter – as they would not survive the freezing temperatures. Note that in the natural world, the ants would reside underground where the temperatures would be a few critical degrees warmer.

Keeping Ants Cool in the Winter

Chapter Fourteen – Ants during the Winter

It is recommended that ants that would normally hibernate, should go into hibernation even if they are kept indoors in a formicarium. Hibernation should ideally be between 3 and 4 months, replicating a normal hibernation period in the natural world. At the very least, hibernation should be offered for one month.

Indeed, many ant experts say that failing to provide hibernation (for at least one month) can result in a shorter life span for the queen and her colony – biologically the queen needs a break from the physical demands of egg laying.

However, there are some ant experts who argue that hibernation is not necessary.

Usually, even in formicarium's that are kept warm during the winter, the ants will go into some form of hibernation. You can expect to see activity levels drop and the level of food intake fall drastically. It certainly appears that the ants are following a biological clock – as well as observing changes in the environment.

Chapter Fifteen – Amazing Ant Trivia

Most likely you are already hooked on the idea of ant keeping – who could resist such fascinating, diverse and unique creatures? For those of you who are still hungry for more, here is a compilation of extraordinary ant facts that you can share with family and friends – just so you can wet their appetite too!

- **Ants have two stomachs.** One stomach is used to digest their own food. The other is a social stomach. The worker ants use their social stomach to store food that they are carry back to the colony. This extra food will provide nourishment for other ants in the nest – the queen, larvae and alates. This is like bees who also have two stomachs (for this same purpose).

- **Ants are super strong.** They can lift items many times their own body weight – as much as 50 times!

- **Lengthy Lifespans.** Ants have the longest lifespans of all other insects.

  Although the female workers and even more so the male drones have a comparatively shorter lifespan, queens can live for up to 30 years – in their natural habitat as well as in captivity.

- **An astounding number of different ant species** that we know of – around 12,000! Ants exist on every continent except for Antarctica.

- **Ants use their legs to detect vibrations** from the ground. These vibrations are so minute that humans and most other animals would not notice or be able to detect such vibrations.

  Ants can determine how large the vibrations are and can identity the direction from which the vibrations are coming from. This alerts the ants to any potential predators or threats.

- **Poor eyesight** means that ants rely on their antennae to navigate. Some species have developed such advanced communication through their antennae that they have no need for eyes at all. An example is the major worker from the Driver ant species.

- **Lazy worker ants within the colony!** Incredibly, some of the worker ants do not contribute anything to the colony. Most worker ants are always occupied with foraging and looking after the queen and brood. In stark contrast, as many as a quarter do not help! They simply crawl around the nest and watch the other ants doing all the work.

- **Ants are efficient farmers.** Ants are the only other animals that have learned how to domesticate other organisms. Whilst humans farm cows, sheep and chickens, ants have domesticated aphids for honeydew. Ants protect the aphids from other insect predators and in return, the ants consume the honeydew that they excrete.

  Sometimes, ants will even take the aphids into their own colonies.

  However, this relationship appears to have a very dark side – ants have been known to clip the wings off the aphids to stop them from flying away – ants have also been known to use chemicals for the same effect.

  Farming is generally considered to be the beginning of modern civilization – and ants mastered husbandry long before humans.

- **Phenomenal excavators,** ants move around 50 tons of soil per year in one square mile.

- **Army ants are nomads.** Without a nest to provide protection and a place to store food, the army ants are permanently on the move.

  By day, the army ants travel en masse, attacking and consuming all other insects in their path. At nightfall, they make a temporary nest that provides shelter overnight.

- **Immense colonies** can be constructed by ants – with no real leadership and certainly no blueprints.

  The greatest colony was found in Argentina. Over 6000 km (3750), it is the same length as the Great Wall of China. This was the home to millions of queens and billions of worker ants.

  The nest began as a group of smaller ant colonies which amalgamated to become one colossal super colony.

- **A practical approach to death,** ants will drag out any dead ants and remove them from the colony. When an ant dies, it emits a pheromone that alerts the other ants.

This approach ensures that the ant colony is kept clean and free from decay – and decreases the chance of disease spreading.

- **Self-exploding ants** as a last resort means of self-defense.

  Some species of carpenter ants will explode if under immense threat. As the ant explodes, it covers its attacker in destructive chemicals – this self-sacrifice will help to defend the rest of the colony.

- **Ants breathe oxygen through their bodies.** The body of an ant is covered in miniscule holes, known as spiracles. Oxygen flows into the spiracles and carbon dioxide flows out.

- **Ant population heavier than human population.** There are just so many ants everywhere that their combined weight is heavier than the combined weight of humans.

- **Some ant species use slavery.** Some ant species will invade other colonies and bring back eggs or larvae to their own colony. These are sometimes consumed – but sometimes force to join the colony as part of the workforce.

Queen ants sometimes also indulge in slavery. The queen will sneak into the nest of an established colony. She will locate the residing queen, attack and kill her – and then take over as the nest's queen. She will use the workers to raise her own brood and look after her - eventually the original workers will be replaced by ants from the new queen.

- **The myth of the leaf cutter ants.** Most people assume that leaf cutter ants forage, cut and drag back leaves to their colony for their own consumption.

  Actually, the diet of the leaf cutter ants is comprised of a fungus that is found within their nest. The ants bring leaves back to the colony to feed the fungus – another demonstration of farming!

- **Power napping ants!** Unlike most other animals, ants have hundreds of micro naps everyday – amounting to almost 5 hours. In between foraging for food, or nurturing the brood, the ants will take a micro nap.

  Whilst some ants are more active during the day (diurnal), other species of ant are more active at night (nocturnal). During hibernation, some ants may sleep for around four months!

Chapter Fifteen – Amazing Ant Trivia

- **As old as dinosaurs,** scientists estimate that ants existed on our planet an incredible 110 to 130 million years ago, in the mid-Cretaceous period. This compares dramatically to humans who are thought to have been on earth for 200,000 years.

- **The largest ever ant** to be discovered was about 6 cm long with a wingspan of about 15 cm. Of course, this species does not exist today – it is a fossilized specimen that belongs to *Titanomyrma giganteum.*

- **Ants underwater,** can often survive for around 24 hours. This is because of the spiracles, small holes that are found all over their body. As long as the water is evaporating, oxygen will be able to flow into the spiracles, keeping the ant alive.

  There are some, although very few, ant species that can actually swim!

- **Controlled gliding** is used by some species of wingless ants that are native to tropical rain forest canopies. When they fall from the tree tops, they are able to use a controlled glide to return to their nest in the tree trunk. This prevents them from falling to the forest floor where they would be under threat from predators.

Chapter Fifteen – Amazing Ant Trivia

- **Ants are regarded as a culinary delicacy** in some parts of the world.

  The Mexican dish 'escamoles' is mainly comprised of the pupae of some species of ants.

  In some regions of India, they are viewed as a form of insect caviar and can sell for as much as $40 per lb.

  The green weaver ant is used as a condiment with curry throughout Burma and Thailand – here it is also added to a salad named 'yum'.
  In North Queensland, Australia, natives mash up ants in water to make a drink that is comparable to lemon squash.

- **Ants versus Ants.** The biggest threat to ants is probably other ants from different colonies. Ants regard each other as enemies. They will team up with ants from their own colony to defeat their opponent – ants will use their mandibles (jaws) to hold the antennae or legs of their victim while their teammates tear the victim apart.

  The victorious ants usually invade the conquered colony and take away the brood - either for food or to become slaves within their colony.

Chapter Sixteen – Afterword

Ants are undeniably fascinating – both in the natural world and within the formicarium. Whether you can capture your own queen or buy a queen, you are in for an incredible journey.

This is your opportunity to observe, up close, the way ants build up their colony – right from the very beginning with just one solo queen until you have an entire colony with thousands of workers.

Chapter Sixteen – Afterword

It's an incredible privilege to be able to watch these industrious creatures at work. Be a witness to their complex social infrastructure that will never cease to amaze.

Get your test-tube nest set-up and you will soon be on your way. There are numerous online forums available to support you; whether you are a beginner or an expert. Utilize these - ask any question that you need answering. You will find that other ant enthusiasts are always very keen to help you out.

Once the formicarium is set-up, ants are relatively low maintenance – giving you the flexibility to try out other colonies and other species. Not only that, you will be able to keep them alongside any other pets that you have.

The most challenging issue is achieving the correct levels in temperature and hydration. Nonetheless, ants are usually very sturdy and can withstand a little trial and error. Once you have attained the optimum levels, your colony is bound to thrive.

Although an unusual choice, ants are a brilliant choice for adults as well as children. The more you think about it, the question becomes one of 'when can I' rather than 'shall I'.

Ant keeping is an exceptionally rewarding experience, something truly spectacular and special that you can make part of your life.

Glossary

Please note this is not an exhaustive glossary of ant-related terminology. The following words have been defined in an effort to augment the existing text and to provide a novice ant keeper with a working vocabulary.

A

Abdomen – Also called the gaster, the abdomen houses the vital and reproductive organs, including a heart and digestive system. Some species also carry stingers on the backs of their abdomens.

Glossary

Alate – A female queen ant or a reproductive male ant.

Antennae – The most crucial sense organ for the ant. They are used to smell, touch, feel and communicate with other ants.

Aphids – small sap sucking insects

Army ants – These include over 200 ant species who are distinct for their aggressive predatory foraging techniques. They carry out "raids" where huge numbers of ant's forage simultaneously over a particular area. Also unique is that army ants do not construct permanent nests.

Austin, Frank Eugene – The first commercially sold formicarium was introduced around 1929 by Frank Eugene Austin.

B

Bivouac – Army and driver ants sometimes form nests with their own bodies to protect the queen and larvae.

Black Garden Ants - *Lasius Niger*, common throughout North America, South America, Europe, Asia and Australasia.

Brood – Eggs, larvae and pupae.

Brood Boosting – Where ants steal eggs, larvae and pupae from another nest and place them in their own nest. The aim is to boost their own numbers, thereby expanding the colony.

Brood Parasites – Slave making ants that capture broods of other ant species to increase the worker force in their own colony.

C

Carpenter Ants – *Camponotus.* Comparatively large ants that are indigenous to many forested parts of the world. Nests of the Carpenter ants are built inside wood.

Colony – The highly organized society where ants live and organize their lifecycle. Colonies can be comprised of just a few individual ants or can consist of millions of individual ants.

Camponotus – Carpenter Ants

Compound Eyes – Most ants have two compound eyes that contain hundreds of lenses. These combine to form a single image in the brain. See also **ocelli**.

Cuticle – The skeleton of the ant.

D

Division of Labor – The separation of tasks within the colony so that different castes of ant specialize in different functions.

Drone – A winged male ant.

Dufour's Gland – An abdominal gland from which chemicals (pheromones) are secreted.

Dulosis – The practice of slave making ants who capture the eggs, larvae and pupae from other ant species and rear them as workers within their own colony.

E

Egg – First stage in the ant lifecycle. Eggs tend to cluster together in the nest.

Ergate – A member of the non-reproductive working caste.

Exoskeleton – A hard waterproof body covering. It is made of a glucose-based material called chitin. The exoskeleton protects the ant's muscle and soft tissue.

F

Glossary

Fire Ant – This is the common name for several species of ants in the genus *Solenopsis*. Fire ants tend to sting and are often referred to as red ants due to their light brown color.

Fluon – Used to escape proof an open foraging area.

Forager - Worker ants that search for, find and bring back food for the colony to share.

Formic acid - The acid produced by ants. The most common species of black ant in the United States is the black carpenter ant. This ant emits a small amount of formic acid through its jaws as it bites.

Formica fusca – Slave ants.

Formicarium – The home to pet ants. The origin of the word comes from the French word for ants – fourmi. A formicarium can be any shape or size.

Fully Claustral queen – Fully claustral queens do no need feeding or extra nourishment before their initial set of worker ants have emerged.

Fungivores – Feeding on fungi.

G

Gamergate – A female worker ant who has mated and is laying eggs in a species which lacks a queen ant.

Glossary

Gaster – Part of the abdomen. Containing vital organs, it has a telescoping construction of seven sections. This provides this large area with flexibility.

Granivorous – Feeding on grain.

Gyne – A member of the female reproductive caste.

H

Haplometrosis – The establishment of an ant colony by a single queen.

Harvester Ants – The common name for any species of ants that collect seeds, or mushrooms.

Honeydew – Provided to ants by aphids. Sap feeding aphids secrete honeydew which the ants consume.

Honeydew Surrogate - solution of sugars and amino acids, to imitate honeydew. The honeydew surrogate is prepared by ant keepers.

Honey water - Liquid food that provides source of energy for ants. It is made from honey and water.

Humidity – Moisture level within the formicarium.

Hydration –Appropriate humidity levels through provision of water both for consumption and evaporation.

Glossary

Hydrometer – This can be used to measure the moisture level / humidity within the formicarium.

Hymenoptera - The scientific order to which ants belong. Also includes bees, wasps and sawflies.

I

Infra-Buccal – As the ant cleans itself, it collects up dirt and deposits it an infra-buccal pocket. This is situated just below the mouth. When the pocket becomes full, the ant will empty the pocket into an allocated garbage pile outside of the nest.

J

Janet, Charles – Inventor of the first formicarium in the 1900's.

K

L

Larvae – Second stage in the ant lifecycle.

Lasius Niger – Black Garden Ants

Levine, Milton – in 1956, Levine bought ant farms to the market, marking the beginning of their rise in popularity.

Life Cycle – There are four stages in the ant's life cycle – egg, larvae, pupae, adult ant.

M

Mandibles – The ant's jaws; used for cutting, holding, fighting and digging. They have smaller mouthparts for chewing food.

Mating flight – See nuptial flight.

Mesosoma – Middle part of the body – the thorax.

Metamorphosis - Metamorphosis is a four-stage life cycle through which all ants pass. The stages are: egg, larva, pupa, and adult.

Monogyny – A single queen resides in the nest.

Monomorphic – All worker ants are of the same size and are of the same caste. The role of the workers changes as the ant becomes older.

Multi coloniality – Where there are multiple independent colonies situated close together.

Myrmecology – The study of ants.

Myrmica rubra – Red ants.

N

Nanitic – The first generation of worker ants. Ordinarily, they are smaller than later generations.

Nuptial Flight – The flying alates (princesses and drones) fly away from the nest ready for mating. Drones and Princesses mate mid-air.

O

Ocelli – Ants have three simple eyes nestled between their two larger compound eyes. These are called ocelli and can detect light and shadow.

P

Pavement Ants – *Tetramorium.* These ants are native to Europe but have spread to North America. The name 'pavement ant' comes from the fact that colonies in North America primarily make their homes in pavement.

Pheromone - A chemical released by one ant to trigger certain behaviors in another. Ants create pheromones from glands located all over their body. They use their pheromones to communicate with all members of the colony.

Pheromone Trail – A trail of chemical compounds secreted by ants to guide nestmates to a particular location (usually food source).

Polygyny – Where multiple queens reside in the nest.

Glossary

Polymorphic – A colony where there is a variation in the size of the worker ants. Different tasks are assigned to different sized workers - they belong to different castes such as major workers and minor workers.

Pupae – Stage three of the ant life cycle. Pupae look like white waxy ants that lay with their legs and antennae folded up against their bodies.

Q

Queen – A female reproducing ant – generally she is the mother of all the other ants in the colony. The queen is the lifeline of the colony and without her, the colony would soon diminish.

R

Red Ants - *Myrmica rubra*. The name red ant stems from their light brown color.

S

Semi-claustral queen – During the founding stages, semi-claustral queens require a foraging area and access to food.
Slave ants - *Formica fusca*. These are brood parasites that capture broods of other ant species to increase the workforce in their own colony.

Glossary

Slave-Making – The capture of brood from other ant colonies – that are then reared as part of the workforce, hence they are slaves.

Social parasites – A type of queen that is a social parasite. These queens need a host to establish a colony. They typically invade another colony and kill the queen – then use the workforce to raise her own brood.

Spiracles – Miniscule tubes cover the ant's exoskeleton. Air flows through these tubes (spiracles) providing the ant with a source of oxygen.

Stinger – Some species of ants have stingers. These are attached to the abdomen. Stingers are used to inject formic acid into their victims.

Sugar Water – Liquid food providing energy for ants, made from sugar and water.

Symbiotic Relationship – Ants have developed mutually beneficial relationships with other organisms to help them thrive in their natural environment. For example, ants and aphids – ants offer protection and gain honeydew in return.

T

Tandem Running – Some ant species use tandem running as a recruitment method – one ant will lead another nestmate who follows closely behind. The guiding ant will lead them to a destination (normally food source).

Test tube nest – ideal nest for a fertilized queen waiting for eggs / workers to emerge.

Tetramorium – Pavement ants.

Thorax - The middle section of the ant's body, both powerful and muscular. Legs are attached to the thorax. The wings of alate's are also attached to the thorax –these are ordinarily torn off during or after mating.

Trophallaxis – The transfer and sharing of food among ants in the colony.

U

V

Virgin Queen – A queen ant before she has mated.

W

Worker Ants – Female ants that have undeveloped reproductive organs. They will carry out all the tasks within the colony.

X

Index

Y

Z

Index

Abdomen, 28
Alate, 19
Ant farms, 67
Antennae, 24, 36
Aphids, 40
Army ants, 40
Austin, Frank Eugene, 65
Black Garden Ants, 115
Blood, 29
Brain, 29
Brood, 16, 32
Bullet ant, 37
Camponotus, 119, 121
Carnivores, 40
Carpenter ant, 119, 121
Caste, 14
Claustral, 118, 122, 127
Claws, 28
Cocoon, 35
Colony, 14, 47
Common red ant, 130
Communication, 35
Compound eye, 23
Containment, 87
Crop, 29, 42
Cuticle, 22

Defense, 37
Drinking, 26
Drones, 15, 19
Dry nest, 109
Dufour's gland, 30
Egg production, 144
Eggs, 15, 34, 54, 63, 77
Escape proofing, 88
Exoskeletons, 22
Farming, 41
Feeding, 105
Fertilization, 64
Fire ants, 38
Fluon, 92
Foraging, 39, 79
Foraging area, 49, 97
Formic acid, 28, 29, 37, 136
Formicarium, 13, 48, 49, 97, 98
Fully-claustral, 74, 138
Gaster, 28, 64
Gel based, 69
Global Ant Nursery Project, 56, 64
Harvester ant, 18, 106
Head, 23

Index

Heart, 29

Heat pad, 144

Herbivores, 40

Hibernation, 119, 123, 129, 134, 139, 149, 150

Honey water, 80

Honeydew, 41, 117

Honeydew surrogate, 80

Humidity, 108, 109, 112

Hygrometers, 111

Infra-Buccal Pocket, 27

Insects, 105

Invertebrate, 22

Jack jumper ants, 37

Janet, Charles, 65

Larvae, 34

Lasius Niger, 115

Leaf cutter ant, 18, 40

Legs, 28

Levine, Milton, 66

Life cycle, 32

Lifespan, 147

Major workers, 17, 46

Mandibles, 25, 38

Matriarchal, 14

Median Workers, 18

Mesosoma, 27

Metamorphosis, 32

Minor workers, 17, 45

Moats, 92

Mold, 85, 112, 145

Monogamous, 118, 122, 128, 138

Monomorphic, 45, 128

Mouth, 26

Myrmecologists, 13

Myrmica rubra, 130, 131

Nanitics, 16, 78, 105

Nerve Cord, 29

Nests, 14, 100

Nuptial flight, 15, 19, 31, 61

Ommatidia, 23

Omnivores, 40

Pathogens, 38

Pavement Ants, 124

Pesticides, 106

Pheromones, 30, 36

Polygynous, 133, 138, 143

Polymorphic, 17, 45, 123

Princess, 19

Pupae, 35

Queen, 14, 47, 56, 72, 96

Rectum, 29

Red ants, 130

Sand, 68

Seeds, 106

Semi-claustral, 75, 133

Social parasite, 76

Social stomach, 42

Soldier ants, 18, 46

Sperm pocket, 32

Index

Spiracles, 27

Stinger, 28, 126, 131

Stress, 74, 87

Sugar, 79

Sugar water, 80

Symbiotic relationship, 41

Talcum powder, 90

Temperature, 112

Test tube, 79

Test tube nest, 50, 72

Tetramorium, 124

Thorax, 27

Trap jaw ants, 38

Trophallaxis, 42

Uncle Milton industries, 66

Vaseline, 91

Virgin Queen, 19

Water, 146

Winged ants, 142

Worker Ants, 16

Made in the USA
Monee, IL
28 April 2021